THE CRUCIBLE
OF FAILURE

Spring Journal Books

Jungian Odyssey Series

Other Titles in the Series

Intimacy:
VENTURING THE UNCERTAINTIES OF THE HEART, VOL. I
SERIES EDITORS: ISABELLE MEIER, STACY WIRTH, JOHN HILL

Destruction and Creation:
FACING THE AMBIGUITIES OF POWER, VOL. II
SERIES EDITORS: STACY WIRTH, ISABELLE MEIER, JOHN HILL

Trust and Betrayal:
DAWNINGS OF CONSCIOUSNESS, VOL. III
SERIES EDITORS: STACY WIRTH, ISABELLE MEIER, JOHN HILL

The Playful Psyche:
ENTERING CHAOS, COINCIDENCE, TRANSFORMATION, VOL. IV
SERIES EDITORS: STACY WIRTH, ISABELLE MEIER, JOHN HILL, NANCY CATER

Love:
TRAVERSING ITS PEAKS AND VALLEYS, VOL. V
SERIES EDITORS: STACY WIRTH, ISABELLE MEIER, JOHN HILL, NANCY CATER

Echoes of Silence:
LISTENING TO SOUL, SELF, OTHER, VOL. VI
SERIES EDITORS: URSULA WIRTZ, STACY WIRTH, NANCY CATER

JUNGIAN ODYSSEY SERIES • VOLUME VII

THE CRUCIBLE
OF FAILURE

Series Editors
Ursula Wirtz
Stacy Wirth
Deborah Egger
Katy Remark

Consulting Editor
Nancy Cater

SPRING JOURNAL
BOOKS

PUBLICATIONS IN JUNGIAN PSYCHOLOGY
www.springjournalandbooks.com

Published by
Spring Journal, Inc.
New Orleans, Louisiana USA
www.springjournalandbooks.com

Cover Photograph:
The Eiger North Face © 2014 Katy Remark

Cover design and typography:
Northern Graphic Design and Publishing
info@ncarto.com

Text printed on acid-free paper

Library of Congress Cataloging-in-Publication Data Pending

REFLECTIONS

Photograph and Text by Andrew Fellows, 2014
Inspired by audience questions on the film,
Eiger: Wall of Death, shown at the
Jungian Odyssey, Grindelwald 2014

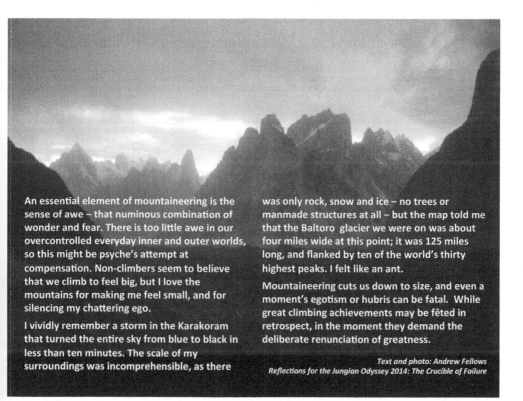

An essential element of mountaineering is the sense of awe – that numinous combination of wonder and fear. There is too little awe in our overcontrolled everyday inner and outer worlds, so this might be psyche's attempt at compensation. Non-climbers seem to believe that we climb to feel big, but I love the mountains for making me feel small, and for silencing my chattering ego.

I vividly remember a storm in the Karakoram that turned the entire sky from blue to black in less than ten minutes. The scale of my surroundings was incomprehensible, as there was only rock, snow and ice – no trees or manmade structures at all – but the map told me that the Baltoro glacier we were on was about four miles wide at this point; it was 125 miles long, and flanked by ten of the world's thirty highest peaks. I felt like an ant.

Mountaineering cuts us down to size, and even a moment's egotism or hubris can be fatal. While great climbing achievements may be fêted in retrospect, in the moment they demand the deliberate renunciation of greatness.

Text and photo: Andrew Fellows
Reflections for the Jungian Odyssey 2014: The Crucible of Failure

Contents

Reflections
Andrew Fellows vii

Acknowledgements xi

Introduction
The Jungian Odyssey Committee 1

Gather Up Your Brokenness:
Love, Imperfection, and Human Ideals
Polly Young-Eisendrath 7

Failure and Success in Forms of Involuntary Dislocation:
Trauma, Resilience, and Adversity-Activated Development
Renos K. Papadopoulos 25

Letting Go of Success
Andrew Fellows 51

Failure is the End
Bernard Sartorius 71

The Implications of Shame for the Analytical Process
Ursula Lenz Bücker 89

On the Role of Failure in the Individuation Process
Murray Stein 105

Even Fairy Godmothers Can Fail
Diane Cousineau Brutsche 121

About AGAP, ISAPZURICH, and the Jungian Odyssey 135

Editors 138

Contributors 142

Acknowledgements

I f it seems unorthodox to begin our acknowledgments with a leave-taking, we find it the apt place to inform our readers that this volume will be the last in the Jungian Odyssey Series. Our immense gratitude for eight years of fruitful collaboration remains with our publisher and friend, Nancy Cater of Spring Journal Books. Indeed for many years Nancy even worked behind the scenes as a member of the Jungian Odyssey Committee, and we especially enjoyed her presence in Grindelwald. Over the years the support from Nancy and Spring contributed substantially to make of the Odyssey a hallmark retreat that gathers so many individuals from all around the world and myriad walks of life. And because we know that attendees and others have valued the Jungian Odyssey Series, as we plan future Odysseys we are exploring other ways of documenting each year's lectures.

As is the case for every Odyssey, so too in Grindelwald the event's smooth running relied on pooled talents. Too many to name here are those colleagues who led the morning meditations and the afternoon seminars and workshops. Helga Kopecky, then librarian of ISAPZURICH, kept us well supplied with titles for our bookshop. Mary Tomlinson, a Canadian analyst and ISAP graduate (2011), continued, as she has done since 2006, to manage the allocation of course preferences. ISAP candidates held forth with remarkable commitment: Sara Liuh assisted attendees with their evolving course preferences; Violetta Milutinovic and Bill Hansen kept apace with book sales; Ashish Pant, Yukiko Higuchi, and Juha Klaavu provided technical support; and Naoko Nakamura served as official photographer, capturing the week in vivid images that can be viewed by following the links on our website: www.isapzurich.com > Program Offerings > Jungian Odyssey > Photo Albums. Last but certainly not least: our young friends and upcoming DJs Catherine Egger and Jessica Pfister provided music for dancing at the closing gala dinner.

Ursula Wirtz, Deborah Egger,
Stacy Wirth, Katy Remark
Zürich, February 2015

Introduction
The Crucible of Failure

Ursula Wirtz and Stacy Wirth

> We must experiment. We must make mistakes. We
> must live out our own version of life. And there will
> be error. If you avoid error you do not live; in a sense
> it may be said that every life is a mistake, for no one
> has found the truth. ... And so the last thing I would
> say to each of you, my friends, is: Carry through
> your life as well as you can, even if it is based on
> error, because life has to be undone, and one often
> gets to truth through error. ... So, be human, seek
> understanding, seek insight, and make your
> hypothesis, your philosophy of life.
>
> —C.G. Jung[1]

Like its predecessors, this final volume of the published series collects the papers of scholars who lectured at ISAPZURICH's annual Jungian Odyssey. They draw on a range of sources and examples—clinical case work, field work with refugees, history, myth, fairy tale, and even mountaineering—and thus appeal to clinicians as well as to all others with interest in C.G. Jung's Analytical Psychology.

For this, our ninth event, the galvanizing *genius loci* beckoned from Grindelwald, a village lying in a green hollow at 3392 feet (1034 meters) in the Bernese Alps. The village itself became a literal cauldron of violent change in 1892, when it was nearly decimated by fire. In 1893 the totally incinerated village smithy provided the foundation of what would come to flourish and become today's romantic Hotel Schweizerhof, our venue. An (in)famous trio of mountains commands the historic setting: the Eiger, the Mönch, and the Jungfrau. As we were all very much aware, if these majestic mountains could speak, they would tell of climbers who risked their lives scaling formidable heights—some to successful ends and others failing tragically.

And so, at this Odyssey, immersed in this numinous place and rather painful topic, the metaphor "shipwreck" obtained particular meaning. Indeed the German *scheitern*, "to fail," is rooted in nautical language, referring to the splintering of wood, the shattering of a ship against cliffs and rocks. With endearing humor our guest speaker Renos Papadopoulos remarked that, had Odysseus's ship been equipped with "good satellite navigation, it would have been just an ordinary journey that everybody … would have forgotten;" but he also noted,

> you have to be really careful about exalting failure when actually it's real. … [W]e need to appreciate that failure is a powerful archetypal image. It implies an elusive and trickstery dialectic; indeed a crucible. Things are churned up there. … Failure doesn't sort of say, "Oh well, that's it." You know, it niggles, it has a motivational something inside it.[2]

Thankfully, there was no shipwreck for the group that joined the boat cruise on the turquoise waters of Thunersee, an icon of Swiss lakes. However, after a two-hour voyage with breath-taking views of the surrounding mountains, the boat docked in Thun—where the journeyers found themselves stranded in a nearly deserted town because the Jungian Odyssey Committee had overlooked the religious holiday that closed all the museums, shops, and most restaurants! Eerie specters of failure resonated with the group that braved the ascent to the "top of Europe" for a close view of the Jungfraujoch, a saddle pass between the Eiger and the Mönch that rises to 11,716 feet (3,571 meters). The trip to this UNESCO site required a ride on a steeply ascending train that rolled through a four-mile-long mountain tunnel. Stops along the way allowed vistas of the soaring mountains and icy glaciers from within the Eiger itself. Fear and trembling were conveyed to all who joined our showing of *Eiger: Wall of Death*.[3] This gripping documentary film allowed us to witness historic ascents of the Eiger's "legendary north face, a near vertical mile of rock and ice, haunted by savage winds and the ghosts of [the] dead…"[4] We were grateful for the question and answer period spontaneously led by ISAP analyst and passionate climber Andrew Fellows, who gave us another metaphorical perspective when he noted,

> Mountaineering cuts us down to size, and a moment's egotism or hubris can be fatal. While great climbing achievements may be fêted in retrospect, in the moment they demand the deliberate renunciation of greatness.[5]

During the Odyssey lectures, seminars, and workshops, there was general agreement that as a collective, we seem bent on attaining Icarus-like heights, geared ever more toward the future, lusting for perfection, dominance, money, and fame. It seems to be built into our collective identity to follow the hubristic ego, and thus to avoid the renunciation of success. We tend to be oblivious to our failures, or we ban them, remaining with hidden guilt and shame. In the *temenos*, a specially protected space and time, we disclosed our personal short-comings, mistakes, and failures—small and large, professional, intellectual, moral, ethical, relational, institutional. Participants asked, which failures reveal our human fragility and vulnerability? What has been the healing power of failure in our lives? We found relief in the convivial, communal meals at our venue. Many of us will fondly remember the dinner concert presented by the gifted Alpentrio, who not only stirred us to a most spontaneous dance. They also allowed the open display of our utter incompetence with their invitation to try our own hands at playing the alphorn. Or to attempt *Talerschwingen*, the deceptively simple alpine art of swirling coins in ceramic bowls. Only the rare beginner succeeds to engender the wistful sound reminiscent of distant cowbells.

The authors in this volume urge the reader to uncover and circumambulate the crucible of failure. Keynote speaker Polly-Young Eisendrath proposes, "Our inherent brokenness provides a primary way to embrace our imperfect species and the imperfect world on which we depend." As if attuning to St. Augustine's thought—*fallor ergo sum*, "I err, therefore I am"—the authors ask for favorable winds that would blow us to the shores of knowledge and wisdom, initiating us into the paradox of failing and becoming.[6] The chapters to come invite the reader to consider that failure might ennoble our humanity, if we can think of it as a turning point, an indicator of a needed paradigm shift. Let us read on, recalling Samuel Beckett's self-minder, "Ever tried. Ever failed. No matter. Try Again. Fail again. Fail better."[7]

—on behalf of the Jungian Odyssey Committee
Ursula Wirtz, Academic Chair
Deborah Egger, Co-Chair
Stacy Wirth, Co-Chair
Katy Remark, Internuncio
Nancy Cater, Honorary Advisor

NOTES

[1] C.G. Jung, "Is Analytical Psychology a Religion?" (1936), in *C.G. Jung Speaking, Interviews and Encounters*), eds. William McGuire, R.F.C. Hull, Bollingen Series XCVII, Third Paperback Printing (Princeton, NJ: Princeton University Press, 1993), p. 98.

[2] Renos Papadopoulous, cited from the unpublished audio recording of his Odyssey lecture, "Failures and Success in Forms of Involuntary Dislocation: Trauma, Resilience, and Adversity-Activated Development."

[3] Steve Robinson, Director, *Eiger: Wall of Death* (UK: Indus Films, 2010).

[4] Sam Walliston, "TV Review: Eiger Wall of Death… ," 2 September 2010, in *The Guardian*, at http://www.theguardian.com/tv-and-radio/2010/sep/02/eiger-wall-of-death-review (accessed 25 January 2015).

[5] Andrew Fellows, spontaneous remarks at the Jungian Odyssey 2014; published in the Front Matter of this volume.

[6] St. Augustine, "The City of God," cited in James M. Byrne, *Religion and the Enlightenment: From Descartes to Kant* (Louisville, KY: Westminster John Knox Press, 1997), p. 58.

[7] Samuel Beckett, "Worstward Ho" (1986), in *Nohow On: Company, Ill Seen Ill Said, Worstward Ho: Three Novels*, 1st Ed. (New York: Grove Press, 1995), p. 89.

1

Gather Up Your Brokenness
Love, Imperfection, and Human Ideals

Polly Young-Eisendrath

The American bard Bob Dylan once sang, "[T]here is no success like failure ... and failure's no success at all."[1] That's a line from his song "Love Minus Zero/No Limit" and the line has stayed in my mind for decades. It pops up at moments when I am doing clinical practice and when I am just walking around. It sounds mysterious and yet, I think I know what it means: that failure has much more impact in our lives than success has. The line evokes in me a respect for failure: what it means and what it teaches.

I want to take this opportunity to introduce myself in terms of the respect I have for failure and the deep resonance of that respect in my work, spiritual practice, writing, and teaching. I am a Jungian psychoanalyst, a developmental psychologist, a teacher of mindfulness, and a long-time practitioner of Buddhism (in the forms of Soto Zen and Vipassana). One reason I was originally drawn to Jung was his belief in the value of brokenness and the ways in which the dark alchemical matter of life's imperfections can be transformed into the priceless gold of wisdom and insight.

Before I found Jung, I found Buddhism. I began to practice Zen in 1970. I grew up in a working-class family in Akron, Ohio, in which I witnessed suffering and violence that went unacknowledged and ignored, as far as I could tell. As a college student barely twenty, I left my childhood religion of Roman Catholicism. Then I made my own search through the religions that were available to me—attending their practices and learning about them and their communities—in order to find one that was grounded in daily life instead of ritual or dogma. I recall that I first came across the idea that a religion could be about daily life by studying indigenous African religions in college. I also wanted to practice a religion that would not ask me to leave my intelligence at the door. Most important, I wanted a religion that was completely honest about the imperfections, losses, and anguish of this world without asking me to assume that I would be saved by finding eternal perfection in an afterlife that seemed childishly contrived.

In 1970, I discovered Zen Buddhism and it seemed to be the answer to my search. I took formal vows in 1971. By 1975, however, I could see that Zen practice was not enough: Many of those leading the practice, and I myself, had psychological problems that were ignored or over-ridden in the atmosphere of intense meditation and deep spiritual inquiry into the moment-to-moment arising of our subjective experience. The practice was leaving out important aspects of our intimate relationships and interpersonal habits, even though it was allowing us to become intimate with ourselves in a transformative way.

And so, I sought out personal psychotherapy that eventually led me into Jungian analysis with June Singer. In 1979, I began to train to become a Jungian analyst. I was in graduate school, at that time, becoming a developmental psychologist. Eventually, I became a professor of developmental and clinical psychology in the Graduate of Social Work and Social Research at Bryn Mawr College, just outside of Philadelphia. At that time, and more and more over the years, I brought the perspective of Buddhist practice and teaching to my understanding of both theoretical and clinical issues within psychoanalysis and psychotherapy (Jungian, object relations, and inter-subjective approaches that I have studied and practiced) and to my teaching of developmental psychology.

By 1994, I had left academic life and was in full-time clinical practice, also engaged in writing and speaking. At that time, I moved from Philadelphia to Vermont and since 2000, I live in a house on the side of a mountain, on about 600 uninhabited acres (although I own only eleven of them). My home is a small retreat center with its own zendo. I have my clinical office there, as well. I participate in, and occasionally lead, Buddhist retreats that have been influenced primarily by Soto Zen Buddhism and Vipassana. My life and community are steeped in Buddhist practice as I live in the most Buddhist state in the US. Many of my closest friends are Buddhist practitioners and teachers. I have become a mindfulness teacher in the tradition of Shinzen Young, my Vipassana teacher. In these recent years, I have also begun to practice the Tibetan teachings on conscious dying called *Phowa*, adding to my practice skills and enlarging my spiritual community.

What I appreciated about Buddhism when I first discovered it, and continue to appreciate, is its emphasis on imperfection, impermanence, and limitation. Buddhism is a religion grounded in reality, not ideals, and it offers a means of experiencing the impermanence and imperfection of this world as transcendent. Gradually I have come to a point of view—beautifully expressed in *The Geography of Thought* by the psychologist Richard Nisbett[2] and in *Tiger Writing* by the novelist and professor Gish Jen[3]—that we, in the West, are primed to believe we can find stability and security in a changing world whereas in Asia, broadly speaking, people are primed to believe they must develop equanimity and fascination with impermanence in a changing world. These are profoundly different starting points for the human psyche and lead to different sensibilities. Some Western theorists, including Jung and a handful of philosophers, began to tap into the Eastern worldview by the mid twentieth century, but none of them fully anticipated the huge cultural shift that has ensued over these last fifty years as Buddhism (as a religion) and Mindfulness (as a secular practice) have grown roots in the West, especially in North America. These roots have largely grown in the soil of psychotherapy and psychology instead of the soil of Western religions.

At the beginning of this development, it seemed as though psychoanalysis would be at the center of this development when D.T.

Suzuki came to influence C.G. Jung, Erich Fromm, Karen Horney, and others. But for the past twenty years or so, it has been cognitive behavioral therapy (CBT) that has paired up with mindfulness in the forms of dialectical behavioral therapy (DBT), acceptance and commitment therapy (ACT), and mindfulness-based CBT. In the past decade, however, many books and conferences have been addressing the similarities and differences between the meditative practices of Buddhism and the contemplative practices of psychoanalytic psychotherapy and psychoanalysis. This interface is especially compelling for me and I have been working with a group of people to develop a series of conferences, with accomplished psychoanalysts and experienced Buddhist teachers, called "Enlightening Conversations"—the first of which was held in New York City in October 2007 and the next of which will be held at Harvard Divinity School in 2015.

There are many directions in which I could take a conversation about Buddhism and psychoanalysis, but today I want to talk about our sensitivity to impermanence, imperfection, compassion, and healing. Those of you who know the music of the Canadian singer and Buddhist monk, Leonard Cohen, may have recognized his lyrics in the title of my paper, which I adapted from his recent song called "Come Healing."[4] "O gather up the brokenness," Cohen writes, providing a poetic opening to a discussion of what are called "The Marks of Existence" in Buddhism and "individuation" in Jungian theory. As in so many of his songs, Cohen is teaching about the healing power of embracing your failures, brokenness, and limitations as the essence of your human nature. Whereas most psychoanalytic approaches would encourage you to *grieve* "The fragrance of those promises / You never dared to vow," Leonard Cohen wants you to celebrate them. They connect you to the vulnerability in yourself and your compassion for humanity. Our inherent brokenness provides a primary way to embrace our imperfect species and the imperfect world on which we depend.

THE NATURE OF REALITY

Buddhist teachings present us not simply with a paradigm of impermanence, but also with some unchanging constraints or spiritual laws, traditionally called "The Marks of Existence." I call them "The

Nature of Reality" because they summarize the primary or universal conditions in which we all exist. The Marks of Existence are non-negotiable; they are not a story about our situation; they are the situation. And so, we learn that it is the nature of our world to guarantee loss and limitation and that goes against our deepest desires and wishes. If we reject this nature because it doesn't measure up to our standards, then we increase our own anguish, hatred, and misery. On the other hand, if we embrace the spiritual laws of our world—*Dukkha*, *Anicca*, and *Anatta*, as they are called—then we live with greater confidence, freedom, and ease because we do not try to achieve the impossible by trying to master conditions that are not under our control.

Let's look first at the condition called *Dukkha*, which is wrongly translated simply as "suffering." The actual meaning of *Dukkha* does not have an English equivalent. *Dukkha* refers to a condition in which we are thrown, like a wheel that rides off its axle or a bone that rides out of is socket. We experience being off-center. Our world here is off-center: Nothing lasts and nothing works perfectly well. Any solution to any problem will eventually become a problem itself. As just one illustrative example, we fought hard to get rid of the insecticide DDT and, as a result of getting rid of stockpiles of it, malaria has again become an epidemic in Africa. Closer to my home, many prisons are being shut down in upstate New York; large numbers of prisoners who were charged with minor drug offenses will soon be released. This seems like a great improvement, but it will also cause a lot of new problems and difficulties for many: Former prisoners (some of who have been incarcerated for decades) will become homeless and find it impossible to secure living-wage jobs—not to mention being absorbed into a community they left long ago. Other residents in those upstate New York towns, who had thought they were doing righteous work as prison guards, will now be out of work with few viable options. These are just a couple of examples of the imperfections of *Dukkha* and the ways in which it is impossible "to get things right" in our relationships, our bodies, our machines, our politics, our cultures, our communities, and our species; this *Dukkha* is not only the result of our ideals and premises for justice and fairness, but it is also the result of the conditions of impermanence and constant change that are built into nature, human and otherwise.

The second natural spiritual law is *Anicca* that does have a good English equivalent: impermanence. Impermanence is always taking place—at levels that are both imperceptible and perceptible. Nothing is stable, secure, or lasting. At a molecular and sub-molecular level, and at a cosmic level, the constant changing around us falls outside of our awareness because our perceptual system is not refined enough to pick it up. But we all notice *Anicca* in our aging. Children grow up and change perceptibly, and we grow old and sag perceptibly. Everyone ages, fades, and passes away, unless they die young or suddenly.

And so, we have to cope with *Dukkha* and *Anicca*—no matter how successful or wealthy we are. Of course, we feel thrown off center by anything from bad weather to a fight with our child or spouse, to flight delays or dementia, health crises, and financial crises. We agonize over bounced checks, gluten sensitivity, hangnails, not to mention schizophrenia, cancer, and Alzheimer's. We are constantly losing what we thought we had—whether it's intelligence, our loved ones, common sense, good looks, someone's love, or property values. This is the nature of *Samsara*—the Wheel of Life and Death.

The third quality of our existence, discovered by the Buddha, is a little harder to recognize and to convey. It contributes both to the anguish and the mystery of our lives. It is called *Anatta* and is often translated as No-Self (An-Atman). This translation is misleading because it conveys the absence of something that never existed anyway. The Vietnamese Zen teacher Thich Nhat Hanh defines *Anatta* as "interbeing" and some people use the term "interdependence." Myself, I like the terms "embedded" or "contextualized" that immediately suggest a problem in seeing something a so-called "thing" set apart. All apparent "things" are entirely embedded in fields of being and they cannot be separated out from those fields; when we try to separate out a tree, a person, a baby, a particle from the context on which it depends, it becomes no-thing. In this universe, we are all at once mixed together within contingencies we do not fully perceive or ever understand. In this way, we are all "out of control." Everyone and everything is embedded in a context of limitless time and space; and so, if you just scratched your left ear and wanted to replay the scene so that you could scratch your right ear, the entirety of the universe of time and space would have to be different. Our context of interbeing can never be shaken off. There is a No-Thingness in our world. No thing is set apart from other things. This means that we are always embedded in circumstances that we cannot foresee and do not control.

In my own personal life, my beloved husband of almost thirty years, Ed Epstein, gradually and insidiously came down with early-onset Alzheimer's disease, starting around 2001. He was in his mid-fifties and handsome and healthy, at that time. Like most families that suffer this illness, we lost all of our financial assets before we knew he was ill; he had taken out and lost many credit cards, and written thousands of dollars of checks to himself, and so on. By the time we had a clear diagnosis when he was fifty-nine, the illness was in an advanced stage, and I lost everything that I had been counting on except my ability to make a living. Ed died in September, 2014, at the age of sixty-six.

The deep context of my life changed dramatically and unexpectedly. My only choice was to accept my new conditions and change my fundamental identity (no longer the wife and partner of my best friend in the world) and to learn from what life was teaching. After I divorced Ed in 2009 (a necessity for Medicaid, the public insurance that has paid for Ed's residential care for more than five years; if we had remained married, the cost of his care would have bankrupted me) and put him into residential care, I went through several years of tasting and touching how everything around me had changed. I was embedded in a new life that I had not wanted or chosen. No amount of railing or self-pity could change anything. *Anatta* had entered my personal life in a dramatic way: Either I would now substantially transform my life to become congruent with my new life context or I would become lost to myself and others through envy, shame, rage, and despair (emotions that are often confused with grief).

Through Buddhist practices, we awaken to the fact that we are both Self and No-Self—a changing subjectivity embedded in a shifting context. We have limited mastery over the circumstances in which we are embedded although we retain a childish desire for omnipotence as part of the human personality. Throughout our lives, we are shaped by and respond to circumstances and contingencies that we did not ask for and do not control. Our ability to live within these constraints—to remain alive and vital even in the most unwanted conditions—will be tested by life whether or not we seek psychotherapy, psychoanalysis, or meditation practice.

JUNG'S THEORY OF INDIVIDUATION

Jung regarded the psychological process of human development—something he called by the name "individuation"—to be the two-pronged capacity to know and accept ourselves as particular individuals with specific childhood complexes, and to know and accept ourselves as being constrained by archetypes, the primary imprints of a specifically human life. Individuation, a development that cannot mature until middle adulthood, requires a decentering from the "just so" world of childhood grandiosity and the belief that we can simply know ourselves through our own individual self-examination (because conscious awareness is constrained by the "ego complex" or the unconscious habits that have carried over from our earliest adaptations). As we come to embrace and understand ourselves in terms of our unconscious complexes and habitual motivations, we come to see that we suffer just as others suffer and that we are compelled in many ways just as others are compelled.

For example, in 1928, in one of Jung's earliest definitions of individuation, he said,

> The idiosyncrasy of an individual is not to be understood as any strangeness in his substance or in his components, but rather as a unique combination or gradual differentiation, of functions and faculties which in themselves are universal.[5]

As we come to know ourselves as psychological individuals (not simply as material substances like a brain or a body) we see how we are fundamentally human, like everyone else in a way that, as Jung comments, "seems to stand in opposition to self-alienation."[6] In other words, the universal constraints of human life—birth, attachment relationships, separation and loss, the development of consciousness, and finally, death—open a door to our feeling included in the human species and in sympathetic contact with other human beings if we can unfold through the process and accept ourselves (with curiosity and equanimity) under the shifting conditions.

Individuation also leads to an awareness of our own specific unconsciousness with its range of hidden impulses and motivations, as well as our capacities for creative intuition and symbolic meaning. While Jung sometimes talked about individuation beginning at birth, he mostly described it as a possibility that opened up in midlife through a "self-division:" In our limitations and failures we come to recognize that we are not who we thought we were. We have to surrender our ideals to become a hero in our own lives. By midlife, for example, we may feel we are inherently broken: That we can be unintentionally mean, self-protective, furious, stupid, and so forth. Through the failures of childish omnipotence and grandiosity—if we can recognize them—we recognize that we are deeply neurotic beings.

Jung called this reckoning "the purpose of neurosis." Our fragmented identity and failed ideals wake us up. In adolescence and early adulthood, we may feel powerful, exceptional, and unique, but our individuality is a mask, a type of pretending, as we take up conscious roles and identities (whether in a formal way like becoming a parent or an informal one like being a rebel), that make us feel set apart from others, either cursed or blessed. This feigned individuality admits little of our hidden impulses and our deepest desires. Alongside this "persona" is a dissociated set of motivations and fantasies that Jung called the "shadow complex." This shadow is what we particularly disavow in ourselves, but project and evoke in those who are closest to us.

The first step of individuation in adult life is breaking our identification with the persona and recognizing that we do not know ourselves. We cannot embrace ourselves or become responsible for what we say and do if we do not know who is speaking or acting. Usually this first step is experienced in a breakdown or a break-up (e.g. a divorce or losing a job), and that failure breaks open our initial identity, presenting us with the opportunity for a more complex sense of ourselves. Neurotic conflicts, with their anxieties and depressions, break through our inflated or deflated sense of self. These conflicts, whether they occur within us or within our relationships, force us to see that we are less noble or less understandable than we had previously imagined.

As we follow the path of our individuation, with the help of psychotherapy, analysis and/or spiritual practice, four things should become obvious unless we are deceiving ourselves: (1) that we have multiple centers in our personality that are motivated in ways that are hard to recognize, but can begin to be seen by examining and discovering what we have projected into others and how we react to those projections; (2) that our nighttime dreams and daytime fantasies contain seeds of wisdom that arise from a source that is outside our ordinary awareness; (3) that we have some kind of purpose or work or engagement with life that we need to find by actually trying things, but cannot be forecasted simply from our ideals or desires; and finally (4) that we are responsible for our actions and speech even though they are not fully under our control and often feel driven by our reactivity or feelings. In other words, we come to feel more out of control, and cast about, as we also come to see that we have ourselves caused a lot of the personal difficulties that we previously thought were caused by others. In a certain way, we feel more broken than we did before we started individuating! When we expand this view to include other human beings, we may feel that we are caught in a tragic and uncaring world. But from another perspective, we begin to awaken our love and compassion through just such knowledge.

HUMAN LOVE

Human love, whether it is for your child, parent, partner, sibling, or yourself, is grounded in the knowledge of its object—in the particularity of the individual, the person. In order to love someone, we have to know that person well and to accept her or him without (mostly) wanting to change the person. I have just finished writing a book about love—asking myself the question of what love is. Living within the context of early onset Alzheimer's disease stirred up the question. In writing and researching *The Present Heart: A Memoir of Love, Loss and Discovery*, I saw clearly that human love cannot be explained by reproductive drives, emotional magnetism, sexual desires, attachment bonds, narcissistic reflection, or any kind of biological need.[7] A truly human love is the drive to see our selves in someone else's eyes and to know our selves through someone else's meaning.

Such a love—not shared by other animals—is mysterious and hard to explain, as well as difficult to practice. In order to develop it, we have to trust the other person—or trust our selves if it is self-love—to include our flaws and failures, as well as our virtues and strengths. Contrary to popular opinion, love is not a feeling; feelings come and go, but we expect love to endure as feelings change. Love is an attitude: an on-going fascination with, and pleasure in our beloved, just as he or she is. True love includes a lot of negative feelings, especially hatred when our beloved disappoints and frustrates us, and these feelings have to be subsumed to our dedication to and our interest in the beloved. I think we all have radar for sensing when someone loves us for who we are instead of wanting us to be a narcissistic object, a trophy, or some other version of an Object of Desire.

When love is mutual, on a two-way street, it allows us to transcend our separateness and step out of our self-enclosure. True love requires the skills of empathy, mindfulness, equanimity, emotional maturity, and truth telling. Therapeutic love, the kind we offer in our consulting rooms, is love on a one-way street, but it is love all the same. As I come to know my patients as particular individuals—in the contexts of their flaws, failures, and symptoms—I embrace them with a love that is something like a parental love, rooted firmly in the fact that I can see them in the larger contexts of their lives and meanings. As a result of seeing themselves through my eyes, and having clarified at least some of their hidden meanings and desires, my patients also develop new self-love. And so, we both come to recognize that love requires an embrace of flaws and failures, and is often invited by vulnerability and need.

Mindfulness and Compassion

When people appear in my consulting room—typically feeling like failures in some aspect of their lives—I assume that our joint therapeutic venture will inevitably include the four aspects of individuation I described above. I also assume it will include my coming to love this person as I get to know his or her story through a framework of mindful awareness that naturally awakens my compassion, even though the person may also irritate and frustrate me, as well as engage in negative and idealizing transferences. From a Buddhist perspective, there is no way to come to terms with disruptive and demanding life experiences (our own and others') without the skill of mindfulness. I define "mindfulness" as the combination of concentration and equanimity, a particular kind of awareness that leads to clarity in our perceptions and compassion with our suffering, moment by moment.

The concentration aspect of mindfulness is like the straight spine of our body in sitting meditation. Concentration makes us alert and gathers up our natural awareness so that we can be precisely and pointedly attentive to what is actually going on—which includes what we are thinking and feeling, as well as what we are hearing, seeing, smelling, and so on. Equanimity, on the other hand, allows us to relax and feel a balanced attitude, a matter-of-fact live-and-let-live feeling. When we are practicing mindfulness in a formal way, we take the posture of a straight spine and relaxed limbs, exemplifying concentration and equanimity. Mindfulness is similar to what Freud called "evenly hovering attention." Freud said that psychoanalysts need to pay attention to what is going on in the consulting room in the same way they would pay attention to passing scenery while riding a train: looking at things passing by without particular goals or desires. Freud's description here emphasizes the equanimity aspect of not pushing and pulling on our experience, but allowing it to arise and pass away. This kind of awareness allows us to pay attention even when we are distressed or disturbed; it is the root skill that allows us to work clinically within many stressful and challenging situations.

When it comes to self-love, to befriending yourself, mindfulness permits you to remain interested and connected to the ways you fail to be ideal—the ways you break your own promises, have destructive impulses, and sometimes oppress yourself and others—as well as the ways you meet up to what you want for yourself. In other words, to paraphrase Leonard Cohen, if you take your diamond to the pawnshop, you want to remember how much the diamond is worth, so that you won't trade it for junk. When you feel like rejecting yourself—and your life—it is essential to retain a connection to the worth of a precious human life, as the Buddhists call it. A successful long-term psychotherapy or analysis should restore that sense of worth as a result of acknowledging and including both sides of whatever we judge as positive and negative about ourselves. Jung and other psychoanalysts have often talked about this inclusion as the "reconciling third" between the opposites, the symbol of creative union. For example, Jung says in a letter he wrote to Olga Froebe-Kapteyn in 1945,

> We are crucified between the opposites and delivered up to the
> torture until the "reconciling third" takes shape. Do not doubt
> the rightness of the two sides within you, and let whatever may

happen, happen. Admit that your daughter is right in saying
you are a bad mother, and defend your duty as a mother to
Eranos [the annual Jungian conferences that she organized in
Switzerland].... The apparently unendurable conflict is proof
of the rightness of your life.[8]

Before we can accept both sides of a conflict within ourselves, often
we need to have compassion for ourselves. Compassion is the capacity
to "suffer with" and to abide. Self-compassion allows us to examine
our conflicts without harsh judgment of ourselves or others. I believe
that compassion is built into the human heart: Even the newborn
human infant tries to help its mother. The infant soothes, engages,
or cheers up the mother because the infant depends on her for its
survival. In order to help her, that infant has to notice that she is
suffering. It is the same for ourselves. As adults, we may rationalize
or try to ignore *Dukkha*, our own anguish and lack of balance. And
yet, we have to know that we suffer in order to become
compassionate; if you judge and attack yourself for your limitations
and failures, then you may not feel open to getting help from
psychotherapy or any other form of human understanding. Holding
onto impossible ideals, we can become hostile and sadistic towards
our own and others' limitations and mistakes.

In a successful long-term psychotherapy or analysis, I find that
people eventually become compassionate towards their younger selves,
their family members, their current selves, and often even towards the
entire human species, as they see how lost and confused we all are in
a world that we didn't invent and don't understand.

A brief clinical example will illustrate: a Jewish woman in her early
forties came to see me in psychotherapy. She was a clinical psychologist
and had a lot of superficial insight into her very traumatic family
background. Her father had spent long periods of time in jail for two
bank robberies when she was a child and she had primarily been raised
by her Orthodox Jewish step-mother who was strict and over-worked.
My patient's biological mother had given birth to her when she was
eighteen; her mother was then a hippie who hung around Central Park
in New York City. Her mother also behaved in irresponsible ways, it
was told, in my patient's first year of life. Her mother took
hallucinogenic drugs and eventually had a postpartum psychotic
break. As a result, the court awarded full custody of my patient to her

father when she was about eighteen months old. Father and mother divorced and he had to find other means to care for his little daughter. At first, he placed her with his parents, but then he found a "good woman" to marry, someone he chose for her child-rearing potentials. Eventually my patient was left in the full-time care of her Orthodox Jewish stepmother after her father was arrested by the FBI and taken to jail when my patient was five years old.

Growing up with an overworked stepmother in a strict religious environment was not all bad, but it led to a lot of sneaking around and breaking of rules. My patient idealized her charming father while she attacked and judged her biological mother's "irresponsibility." This narrative remained in place through my patient's early adult life and was the way she told her story at the beginning of her work with me. There is much more to the story—especially about her charming and good-looking father who robbed another bank and had to go back to jail when my patient was eleven, but we will fast forward to her twice per week therapy with me.

About four years into our therapy, the patient was beginning to wrestle with her own relational life; by then, she had her own child and an ex-spouse. She was beginning to approach the notion of getting to know her biological mother who had stayed in touch over the years. As a result of visiting and reaching out to that mother, who was again having occasional psychotic episodes, my patient came to find out the circumstances of her mother's birth: Mother's parents were escaping from a Nazi concentration camp in Poland. Her mother's birth took place in the woods while the family was on the run. In a flash, the patient and I could see that her own birth, when her mother was just eighteen years old, had rekindled the chaotic birth trauma through which her mother had tumbled into the world. Suddenly, it became clear that no one was to blame for the abandonment my patient had suffered. She couldn't blame her mother because she could see how her mother was caught by her circumstances. My patient said, "Should I blame the Nazis for my abandonment or the conditions that brought the Nazis into power?" She could feel the force of *Anatta* in her life; she perceived the context of her life within the larger human context. She felt compassion for her flawed and fragile mother and greater compassion for herself, as well.

THE CRUCIBLE OF FAILURE AND HUMAN WISDOM

My patient gradually began to love her biological mother and to get to know her as a wounded, but caring, human being. Nothing has gone "happily ever after" in this story, but getting to know her "Bio Mom," as we call her, has enriched my patient and her understanding of her own patients. The ways we embrace human failure—our own and others'—will determine a great deal about how satisfying our lives are.

If we see failure as necessary, impossible to avoid, and an element in a vast set of circumstances and contingencies we don't control, then we are a lot less likely to get caught up in harmful narratives of self-pity, revenge, and envy. These are stories of what I like to call "negative self-importance." I gave a *TEDx Middlebury* talk about negative self-importance and so I won't go into the details here.[9] In it, I point out how we have a choice about the way we see our own and others' failures and imperfections: we can get involved in an endless story of blame or shame or we can recognize that no one person (not self, not someone else) is to blame for the circumstances of our lives.

In my *TEDx* talk, I show a modern rendition of a painting in the style of fifth and sixth century Chinese landscape painting. In it there are two very tiny human beings, standing on a steep precipice, looking out at a vast mysterious space. We can imagine that they are telling each other stories about what they see. But they have a choice: they can get caught up in the stories about their small selves (as the Chinese painters want to show us) or they can remain fascinated and amazed by the circumstances in which they find themselves. When you get caught up in the small self stories, you are caught in the self-conscious emotions that always tend to weave into a narrative of blame or shame—what Jung called "the ego complex."

The self-conscious emotions (shame, envy, pride, guilt, jealousy, self-pity, embarrassment) motivate the ego complex, moment-by-moment. They are all uncomfortable and contractive feelings—even pride, as it turns out. People don't enjoy feeling pride because it quickly turns into embarrassment. When you can mostly let the self-conscious emotions slide away, moment-by-moment, then you can begin to feel and see the amazing mystery of your particular life, even in the midst of your responsibility, pain, and anguish. Later in the song, "Come Healing," Leonard Cohen says, "Behold the gates of mercy in arbitrary space, / And none of us deserving the cruelty or the grace."[10] This is the attitude that comes from the crucible of failure: we recognize that the gates of mercy are always open, and that while none of us deserves either the cruelty or the grace of life, the two are always combined in our experience. Only compassion allows the blame and shame to be transformed into a deep inquiry about the meaning of our lives.

Taking such a spiritual perspective often brings people to ask the question, "What about the cruelty? Can't we end cruelty and make the world a safer and better place?" When I am asked this question, I usually answer with another question: "How are things going in your family?" I don't know how or why this world came into existence, or why the cruelty is combined with the grace, but I do know that the Buddhist Marks of Existence are accurate. If we pay close attention to *Dukkha*, *Anicca*, and *Anatta* on an everyday basis, we will remain fascinated with our imperfect lives.

I also know that the way you conduct yourself in your own imperfect life—among those people you are caught up with and those you are supposed to love—will be the key to your getting what you need to go forward, as long as you are not overwhelmed with blame or shame. And I know that our conduct—with our families, our work, and our communities—ripples out into the world at large. It is the same for the compassion and creativity in our consulting rooms and classrooms and businesses. If we want to know what to do about the cruelty of the world, we have to start in our own lives. Recognizing our limitations, failures, and imperfection increases our compassion and modesty, and allows us to stay connected mindfully with our experience.

When I begin the process of a long psychotherapy or psychoanalysis, I often want to say to my patient: The only thing you are going to leave behind, as a result of being here, will be your ideals. Your ideals—whatever they are—exist in a narrative of how things should be: the way family, love, justice, or recycling should be. These ideals interfere with your being deeply interested in and mindful of the way things are. They interfere with your being able to see and use your own failures and limitations to get to know yourself in a friendly and compassionate manner. Your ideals will cause you to freak out, to feel depressed, and be discouraged. Your ideals will encourage you to try to control the people you love instead of accepting them as they are.

As a result of learning to love yourself and perhaps some others, you will have to drop those ideals. And when you do, you will see that your negative opinions and judgments (about others and yourself) actually prevented you from enjoying the complexity of your life. Of course, this does not mean that our plans, desires, and intentions should be dropped. No, we need them very much, but we need to drop the fantasy of perfection or of "measuring up."

We began by quoting the mysterious Bob Dylan who said, "There is no success like failure, and failure's no success at all." I hope you have come to see that our failures and brokenness are the heart of being human and until we recognize them, we cannot truly love. By recognizing them, I mean more than accepting them. With Leonard Cohen, I believe we should celebrate our brokenness because it is what lets in the light. Some of us feel this brokenness too keenly, too harshly, or too soon (in our youngest years), and may then believe that no one can be trusted and nothing should be embraced.

If we become resilient from such childhood adversity, though, we come to discover that it is the brokenness itself—when accepted in a mindful and realistic way—that allows us to tap into our deepest love and compassion.

NOTES

[1] Bob Dylan, "Love Minus Zero/No Limit," Track 4, on *Bringing It All Back Home*, original recording released by Colombia, 1965.

[2] Richard Nisbett, *The Geography of Thought: How Asians and Westerners Think Differently...and Why* (NY: The Free Press, 2004).

[3] Gish Jen, *Tiger Writing: Art, Culture and the Interdependent Self* (Cambridge, MA: Harvard University Press, 2013).

[4] Leonard Cohen, "Come Healing," Track 7, on *Old Ideas*, original recording released by Columbia, 2012.

[5] C.G. Jung, "The Function of the Unconscious," *Two Essays on Analytical Psychology, The Collected Works*, eds. Sir Herbert Read, Michael Fordham, Gerhard Adler, trans. R.F.C. Hull, 2nd Ed., Bollingen Series XX (Princeton, NJ: Princeton University Press, 1977), CW 7, § 267.

[6] *Ibid.*

[7] Polly Young-Eisendrath, *The Present Heart: A Memoir of Love, Loss and Discovery* (Emmaus, PA: Rodale Books, 2014).

[8] Jung, *Letters of C.G. Jung, Vol. 1: 1906-1950*, eds. Gerhard Adler, Aniela Jaffé, trans. R.F.C. Hull, Bollingen Series XCV (London: Routledge, 1973), p. 375.

[9] Young-Eisendrath, "Getting Free of Self-Importance is the Key to Happiness," at "TEDx Middlebury, The Road Not Taken," 2013, *TEDx, independently organized TED event*, at http://tedxtalks.ted.com/video/Getting-Free-Of-Self-Importance;search%3Atag%3A%22TEDxMiddlebury%22 (accessed December 8, 2014).

[10] Cohen, "Come Healing."

2

Failure and Success in Forms of Involuntary Dislocation

Renos K. Papadopoulos

Sweet are the uses of adversity,
Which, like the toad, ugly and venomous,
Wears yet a precious jewel in his head.
—William Shakespeare, *As You Like It*,
Act 2, Scene 1, Lines 12-14

Let me embrace thee, sour adversity,
For wise men say it is the wisest course.
—William Shakespeare, *King Henry VI*,
Part III, Act 3, Scene 1, Lines 24-25

PREAMBLE

In this paper I endeavor to address the theme of failure from what can be essentially considered as a *psychosocial* perspective and also to locate the theme within the context of the different types of activities that I engage in. In addition to being a practicing analyst, I am also an academic, a researcher, and a consultant working with people who have been traumatized by war, political violence, and other disasters. What I value and find particularly enriching is the opportunity—and indeed the privilege—to approach the same subject matter, the same problematic, from a variety of different perspectives and settings, e.g. theory and research, as well as clinical practice within the consulting room and outside of it, doing field work in unconventional and inhospitable terrains.

I will start by examining the theme of failure and looking at some characteristic images that reflect its meaning, scope, and phenomenology. Then, in tune with the Jungian Odyssey conference, I will focus on two specific instances of failure in the context of "involuntary dislocation," emphasizing the meaning of home and the loss of home. That will be connected with the concept of trauma and the wide range of responses to adversity, before I attempt to develop some concluding thoughts. And, of course, if I fail to do all this, then the spirit of failure will properly prevail... !![1]

FAILURE: IMAGE AND SCOPE

A cursory perusal of a range of sayings about failure in popular culture can be very revealing. Here is a sample:

- I like failure because it's SO easy to achieve. (Unknown)
- Nothing succeeds like failure. (Tommy Lasorda)
- Failure defeats losers, inspires winners. (Robert T. Kiyosaki)
- Make failure your teacher, not your undertaker. (Zig Ziglar)
- If you stumble make it part of the dance. (Unknown)
- Failure is an event, never a person. (William D. Brown)
- It is impossible to live without failing at something, unless you live so cautiously that you might as well not have lived at all. In which case, you fail by default. (J.K. Rowling)
- Failure is not falling down but refusing to get up. (Chinese Proverb)
- Failure is simply the opportunity to begin again, this time more intelligently. (Henry Ford)
- Success consists of going from failure to failure without a loss of enthusiasm. (Winston Churchill)

- Failure is not the opposite of success, it is the stepping stone to success (Ariana Huffington)
- We must be willing to let go of the life we have planned so as to have the life that is waiting for us. (Joseph Campbell)
- Trying is the first step toward failure. (Homer Simpson)

Most of these sayings and aphorisms convey the clear message that failure is not necessarily a momentary negative outcome, but it can and perhaps should be conceptualized as part of a process. This process can indeed be the crucible within which failure becomes a catalyst to the transcendence of an existing state and enables a new perspective to emerge. However, this is not the usual way that failure is understood and experienced. Most typically, failure is simply assumed to refer to a negative outcome; an attempt that missed the desired target; a disaster or catastrophe; a process with an unproductive, destructive, and shameful end. This observation should alert us immediately to conclude that failure tends to activate a range of possibilities between the opposites of the ultimately positive and the ultimately negative.

If we attempt to discern the theme of failure in the wider cultural images around us, the results can be astonishing. To begin with, we could argue that the entire Bible could be understood as the attempt to redress an original failure. Adam and Eve are expelled from the Garden of Eden because they fail to adhere to God's command not to eat from the Tree of Knowledge.

The end of the Christian Bible takes place again in a garden, in another garden, the Garden of Gethsemane, where Christ redresses Adam and Eve's failure by obeying (unto death!) God's will. Voluntarily, Christ suffers utter humiliation and crucifixion in order to undo the original failure. In a sense, the Bible conveys that without Adam and Eve's original failure, human life as we know it would not exist. Christ comes to reconnect human life with divine life by doing precisely the opposite of what Adam and Eve did. His death and resurrection create human rebirth and transformation.

Another powerful theme of failure is depicted by the Homeric *Odyssey*, which connects directly with our conference theme. Viewed from the perspective of this paper, Odysseus' entire odyssey takes place as a result of a series of failures. Had he had a satellite navigation system and a more reliable vessel, he would have promptly returned to his

Figure 1. *Adam and Eve in the Garden of Eden*, Lucas Cranach the Elder, Oil on Panel, 81 x 114 cm, 1530 (Art History Museum, Vienna).

Figure 2. *Odysseus*, Roman Mosaic, Third Century
(Bardo National Museum, Tunisia).[2]

beloved island of Ithaca, having finished an ordinary journey that nobody would have known about. But, precisely because of his repeated failure to arrive home as planned (also due to some trickstery obstacles thrown in by the gods), his arrival was delayed and his wanderings produced not only pain and suffering but also a great deal of wisdom and transformation. C.P. Cavafy's famous poem "Ithaca" illustrates this specific point most eloquently. It starts by declaring boldly and paradoxically that, *"If you set out for Ithaca / hope your voyage is a long one, / full of adventure, full of discovery."*[3] An easy and quick journey back home, without adventure and anguish, cannot possibly produce substantial benefits or transformation. It is precisely the failure of such a smooth return that enables wisdom to be gained.

The Phoenix represents another image of failure. Unless the Phoenix dies and is reduced to ashes, he will not be reborn. It is out of his utter destruction, his very own ashes that rebirth takes place.

Figure 3. "Fenix Auis Vnica," Michael Wolgemut, Wilhelm Pleydenwurff, Woodblock, Foliü CIIII, in Schedel Hartmann, *Liber Chronicarum*, 1493 (Bavarian State Library).[4]

The universal and diachronic appeal of this image is testified by the winner of the Eurovision Song Contest 2014, namely the song "Rise like a Phoenix," sung by Conchita Wurst.[5]

Moving on to the psychotherapy realm, we encounter another significant image of failure, which although not so self-evident, is nevertheless extremely relevant. Donald Winnicott's "good enough mother" is based on the fact that she *must* fail. Why? Because if the mother does not fail, she would continue to live symbiotically with her infant, anticipating and fulfilling all of his/her needs. The infant's very development and unfolding awareness of his/her own individuality depends on the mother's failure. For only through this way can the infant experience its own needs and appreciate its separate existence from mother. In Winnicott's own words,

> ... a mother is neither good nor bad nor the product of illusion, but is a separate and independent entity: The good-enough mother ... starts off with an almost complete adaptation to her infant's needs, and as time proceeds she adapts less and less completely, gradually, according to the infant's growing ability to deal with her failure. Her failure to adapt to every need of the child helps them adapt to external realities.[6]

In a similar vein, the influential British psychologist Tanya Byron warns against a serious problem we face today: within our current culture, children are no longer allowed to fail. This is a serious problem. She argues that, "'...risk-taking is important because it helps children to accept, understand, and *embrace* failure.'"[7] Lacking a real and lived appreciation of the positive function of failure, we are brought up with a tyrannical and crippling obsession with success, which makes us unfit to face real life with its inevitable mixture of successes and failures.

The brief examination of these images would justify the claim that failure is, indeed, a powerful archetypal image. Failure engenders an elusive and trickstery dialectic with an evident bi-polarity: on the one pole is the good and transformative failure that creates opportunities, is productive, and enables renewal; this is opposite to the other pole, with its completely antithetical function—the negative failure that destroys creativity, frustrates all efforts, and leads to nothing but catastrophic and disheartening disasters. Are we then to assume that there are two types of failure? Or, are there two polarities of the one and the same phenomenon? Is there a productive and a destructive failure? Or are these two different conceptualizations of one entity with two poles, resulting from the specific epistemology of failure that we adopt? In order to answer these questions, it would be imperative to expand the perspectives of our enquiry.

The first observation that needs to be made is that failure activates its own reconstruction and revision; failure germinates a motivational impulse. Regardless of its direction, the very experience of failure affects us, inevitably, definitively—whether it spurs us to intensifying efforts, transformational re-direction, or drags us into apathy. Failure touches us deeply, it forces us to reconsider our existing positions, our prevailing beliefs, our priorities, our goals and methods of working towards achieving them, it urges us to reconsider our very identity, it forces us to take a stand and decide what to do next. This is the very crucible of failure. It is within this crucible that a person develops his or her own self-perception; it is here that a substantial part of one's very identity is churned and forged. Understanding failure in this way inevitably leads us to develop a new conceptualization of the space (the psychological, but also the geographical, the cultural, etc.) within which this process takes place. I will propose that home is the image and reality of an intimate and safe space, *par excellence*, which provides the best possible framework within which to experience and assess failure, the crucible within which the uniqueness of our personality begins to be formed.

HOMER'S ODYSSEY

The Homeric *Odyssey* is of particular importance in examining the theme of failure for two reasons. Firstly, as already noted, the *Odyssey* represents a timeless theme of endurance and resilience in response to failure, and, secondly, it is one of the most universal dramas that depict the images of home and homecoming. Thus the *Odyssey* offers one of the most potent archetypal imaginings of the trials and tribulations of involuntary dislocation. The theme of home is pivotal in my own work (mostly outside my consulting room) with involuntarily dislocated persons, i.e. those who have been forced to abandon the locations they consider home, due to a wide variety of upheavals, e.g. political, climatic, environmental, etc.

To begin with, it is important to examine how Homer represents home. Very early in the epic, we read that Odysseus is yearning to return, and "...*Odysseus, who would give anything for the mere sight of the smoke from his own land, can only yearn for death...*"[8] Odysseus was dying to see the smoke rising from his own land. That's what he wanted to see, to confirm the end of his struggles, to mark the end of his journey. So Homer is using two opposite elements to describe home: smoke and land—smoke, a most intangible entity, and land, a most solid substance. It is interesting that the word Homer chooses here is not "house" or "household." Although the word *oikos* (*ecos*) exists in Homeric language and is used elsewhere in the *Odyssey*, here he chooses to use the most basic and primal word—*gaia*, "earth," "soil," "land."

Ecos—the root of words like ecology, economy—refers to an "organized household," whereas *gaia* is the most given, the *sine qua non* of any home. Homer, in a most skillful way, places home between the polarities of tangibility and intangibility. In doing so, he gives us the right to consider home as perhaps the most basic archetypal image of human destiny. Moreover, his unique combination of this particular bi-polar set provides us with some hints about attempting to define what home is. The smoke in this passage unmistakably suggests an inhabited land and an actual home where people live. The allusion to the hearth, in Greek *hestia*, is crucial as it refers to the goddess Hestia, the protector of homes, domesticity, and family. It is characteristic and indicative that Hestia—although she is one of the first Olympians—always shuns visibility. She is always in the background, keeping the home fires burning, and in her unassuming and modest way she provides the backbone of the home. It is the hearth that suggests the house is lived in, that it is inhabited by people who gather around the fire for its provision of warmth and light, and the sharing of company, relationships, and cooked food. Little wonder that drawings of home, especially children's drawings, typically show a smoking chimney as an indispensable part—and this, despite the fact that, nowadays, many homes no longer have hearths, much less do they have smoking chimneys.

I would argue that the subject of home has been undergoing a Hestia-like treatment, for although home is so fundamental to human existence and destiny, it seems to be taken for granted. It is truly astonishing that academic disciplines and therapeutic training programs have so long neglected to systematically study or research a reality so basic, vital, and essential as home. Granted, the notion of home may be found in ideas such as Bowlby's "secure base," the Jungian "Self," and Erikson's "psychosocial identity," yet none of them capture the actual uniqueness and complexity of the phenomenon. The meaning of intimate spaces has become the topic of more recent interdisciplinary studies initiated within the realm of Human Geography, which has led to the development of new fields such as "emotional geography" and "place attachment." Original and refreshing contributions from within analytical psychology are exemplified by John Hill's *At Home in the World: Sounds and Symmetries of Belonging*,[9] and by the collection of essays in *On Home and the Wanderer*, the thematic issue of *Spring Journal* Vol. 85, 2011. However, it remains that the subject of home is not yet part of standard academic or training curricula. Home, like Hestia herself, seems to succeed in shying away from the searchlight of formal investigation.

Homer should be credited for providing us with substantial reflections about the nature and impact of home and homecomings. For example, I propose to discern three sets of homecomings in the *Odyssey* that, consequently, suggest three corresponding sets of failures:

(a) Odysseus leaves home and for ten years he is fighting in Troy; then, it takes him another ten years to return home. It should not be forgotten that homecoming begins the very moment one leaves home in search of something new, and the return is not only activated when one is explicitly heading back toward home. Any form of involuntary dislocation includes the movement *from* home and *to* home, and both need to be appreciated as parts of the same process.

(b) Contrary to our expectations, perhaps, Odysseus arrives home in Ithaca not at the end of the epic but exactly in the middle of it. This challenges the commonly held understanding of the term "odyssey" as referring to a purely external adventure that ends with a return to the point of origin. Surely, the *Odyssey* cannot be only about the first half of the poem that addresses Odysseus's geographical journeys and endless trials and tribulations outside Ithaca. The suggestion from Homer is that the external struggling is only one part of an entire odyssey. In the second half, we read of Odysseus's struggles with how *to be* at home. He no longer fights against the elements, monsters, and foreigners, but against his own countrymen, trying to regain his lost position, his royal throne. He uses all his cunning, wisdom, interpersonal skills, and sensitivity to relate to his wife and to re-establish his position within his own family, within his own palace, and within his own country. The *Odyssey* does not end in a triumphant homecoming with the embrace of a welcoming wife aglow in a romantic sunset and the melodic strains of a lyre. The second half of *Odyssey* is as hard, if not harder, than the first.

(c) The third set of homecomings that I propose to identify in the *Odyssey* is less noticeable but equally important and it refers to the actual *direction*. Odysseus is returning "back" home, but the movement is not simply a *backward* one. With reference to time and place, and to overall values, psychological states, and even to socio-political setting, the movement is equally (or even more so) a *forward* one. There is a slippery dialectic here. Definitely, he is returning "back" home but that home is very different from the one he left behind when he embarked to fight in Troy. Everything he encounters on his return to Ithaca is now different and new—his family and relationships, the political situation; even the physical landscape changes after twenty years. Therefore, the movement is both backwards and also forwards; Odysseus is returning to the familiarity of home but he has to develop a new familiarity with a changed and thus new home. He is returning to the locus of origin but, simultaneously, he is also fulfilling his forward aims and aspirations. This is a most significant but, at the same time, difficult reality to grasp about homecomings.

Consequently, we can now identify three corresponding types of failures:

(a) The failure to grasp the subtleties of the home-leaving/homecoming dialectic can result in reified forms of understanding that confuse the dual nature of each part of the overall process. Every home-leaving in effect also includes homecoming dimensions and *vice versa*. When we embark on a search for a new home or for self-improvement with reference to all possible parameters (e.g. material, spiritual, educational, inter-personal), we inevitably carry two images of home—the locus of origin but also the locus of our target aspiration. Without an appreciation of this dual, but slippery and confusing nature of home, no home-leaving or homecoming can be fruitful. Beginnings and endings are inexorably involved in a constant cyclical dialectic, as T.S. Eliot's famous poem suggests: "We shall not cease from exploration / And the end of all our exploring / Will be to arrive where we started / And know the place for the first time."[10]

(b) The sharp division that Homer creates between the *Odyssey's* first and second halves echo Jung's division between the first and second half of life, which hold different prospects for one's life tasks and very identity. Accordingly, we may characterize the *Odyssey's* first half as external and the second as internal, and this would not be incorrect. However, this sharp division introduces the need to consider more complexity. It is as if Homer wants to face us with additional types of struggle and potential fulfillment, rather than limit us to the one connected with external adventures, with the mastering of life adversities and visible forms of hostility. More than this, Homer makes us aware in no uncertain terms that Odysseus survives not only using physical power and battle skills, but also with a great deal of *interpersonal* awareness and *inner* strength, focus, and wisdom. In other words, in addition to the *external* odyssey, we should identify at least two other types of odyssey, i.e. the *interpersonal* and the *inner*. These require a host of sensitivities and abilities, such as the capacities to be inter-relational, interactional, systemically-minded, introspective, and reflective. Moreover, we can discern further and finer forms of odysseys relating to socio-political abilities, emotional awareness and balance, etc.

The main point I want to make here is that a proper reading of the *Odyssey* should expand our understanding of what an odyssey is about. In addition to focusing on physical survival and dominance by brute force, we appreciate the multiplicity of other subtler odysseys involved. Homer created not only a block-buster action production. He also introduced, most astutely, a plethora of psychological finesses, suggesting that homecomings require our highly developed faculties for the negotiation of difficult situations that arise with regard to psychological survival and the ability to relate to family and friends, to the community, and to socio-political realities. Ultimately, the requirements for a successful odyssey, for a fruitful homecoming, are not far from those that are involved in developing a more individuated personality.

Therefore, the cardinal failure that emerges here is to fail to grasp the very intricate complexity of the dialectic inter-relationship between all these types of odysseys and, instead, in a reified way, to prioritize one or two of them. This is illustrated when, for example, we set as our life-goal the acquisition of wealth and power, or the completion of our professional training, or the mastering of one skill, instead of appreciating that self-fulfillment involves much more than achieving such tangible goals.

HOME

It is remarkable that the word and image of home attracts possibly a greater number of idealized associations than any other word. For many years, with many different types of groups (educational, cultural, professional, age, gender, etc.) all over the world, I have been asking people to write down the first words that come to their mind when they hear the word "home." The overwhelming majority produce not only positive associations but, most often, idealized ones that typically link home with attributes such as warmth, nurture, protection, safety, security, support, acceptance. All these are, of course, unmistakably, the very characteristics of Hestia. Yet in reality, not a single actual home is ideal and each one includes various combinations and degrees of opposites such as love and conflict, closeness and distance, hopes and disappointments, joys and sorrows. Like every aspect of human life, home is full of complexities that combine welcome and unwelcome facets; yet, home seems to be unique in constellating images of perfection—only one pole of the human reality. This is an astonishing paradox: although in actuality all homes combine positives and negatives, the image of home almost invariably activates dominantly positive and, indeed idealized attributions.

This would justify our claim that home is in a sense a "magic" word, which we often use to activate the idealized Hestian pole. Among the endless examples all around us is the seduction of so-called "home-made" food products prepared with "home recipes"—while we know full well that a fruit jam produced and bottled in a mass-production plant cannot be home-made. Similarly, the image of home is used to soften the impersonal feel of institutional "care" by calling establishments for the care of children or of the elderly "homes." Other examples include naming state protection as "Homeland Security." Wherever the image of home is evoked, a powerfully positive and idealized archetypal fascination tends to be activated and this is used (and abused) widely because it always seems to work—despite the fact that in many if not most contexts the notion of home is tenuous, far-fetched, or often completely false and untrue.

Another aspect of the magic derives from home's elusive nature, which can make it so difficult for us to pin down its intended meaning. When we talk about home, we tend to confuse its *concrete* and *abstract* constitutive dimensions with its specific and general connotations. All seem to appear in unpredictable combinations. Invariably, when referring to home, we move from the *concrete* to the *abstract*, from the *ideal* to the *real*, without being aware of these shifts. For example, when involuntarily dislocated refugees talk about home (be it their relinquished home of origin, their present home, or their intended home), it is difficult to discern whether their narratives express idealized or reality-based memories and expectations. As a result of the intrinsic complexities and the difficulty in differentiating them, many different kinds of failures are likely to be experienced in this type of work. And the failures are not limited to those in inter-personal communication but also include failures in epistemological conceptualization and self-perception. The elusive, trickstery nature of home strengthens my claim that home is one of the most powerful archetypal images in human life.

So, what is home? How can we define home? In the absence of any set and established academic or professional definition, I draw from my reflections on my work over the years in this field. On this basis I would propose that home could be understood as the dynamic archetypal system, a systemic hub, a network, a cluster, a container of complex inter-relationships between (a) space, (b) time, and (c) relationships. This means that the experience of home emerges whenever specific relationships are established over a period of time and within the context of a particular space.

The space is not limited to geography, physical place, or architecture; it also refers to any space that is experienced as being intimate, and it extends to the sense of space understood in various contexts such as cultural, spiritual, historical, psychological, societal, financial, ethnic, political, and climatic.

Time is neither defined nor limited by its duration. Even within the context of a relatively brief period of time it is possible for one to feel at home, provided that specific relationships are enabled within a particular intimate space. The duration would suffice as long as it enables us to experience over the course of time some changes, some particular repetitions, and some particular patterns.

Finally, although the relationships are primarily between persons, the sense of home also emerges in relationship with objects, events, landscapes, climate, narratives, etc.

Understood and defined in this way, inevitably, home is closely interlinked with a person's identity.

IDENTITY AND NOSTALGIC DISORIENTATION

There is a plethora of theories about identity and all of them are very useful, lending important insights. For the purposes of this paper, I propose a simple model of identity that intends to assist us with the elaboration of the themes addressed here. My proposition is that our personal identity consists of two parts that fit together in a unique way. The first part inheres in the cluster of characteristics that we are mainly aware of; it includes everything that we would each consciously identify as the unique features marking us as individuals. This is the visible part of our identity, with all the *tangibles* such as gender, age, physical and psychological characteristics, abilities, profession, family status, social and financial status, political and ideological beliefs, religious affiliation, activities and hobbies, culture, nationality, ethnicity, wider belief systems, aspirations, one's own body, etc. Most of us would have no problem in consciously naming and appropriately addressing changes in this realm. However, my argument is that this cluster is not the entirety of our identity, but only the visible and *tangible* part.

The tangible part of our identity fits on top of a base, which itself consists of a variety of different elements that are certainly less noticeable, less tangible. The best way to represent them would be in the form of a mosaic, i.e. different elements that together form a pattern and unique fit, a set of diverse pieces that together form a specific design (Figure 4).

This I call the *mosaic substrate of identity* and it is composed of groups of elements such as,

- Sense input: the visual (landscape, nature, architecture, people, artefacts); sounds (natural, human-made, human voices, language, music); smells (natural, human-made); tastes (food, drink, air); touch, feel (textures, clothes)
- Rhythms, habits, rituals: conscious and unconscious
- Sense of belonging: to a home, to a family, community, culture, to my body, to a country (that exists and I have access to it)
- Combinations of dimensions: space, time, relationships

This substrate is extremely important, especially because we tend not to be aware of its existence as a contributing factor to our identity.

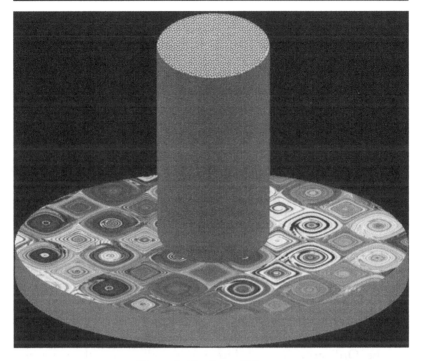

Figure 4. *Two Parts of Identity.*

We take it for granted, as our tendency is to observe and name only the tangible parts. We constantly underestimate the importance of this mosaic substrate in forming our identity—but we definitely become aware of it when certain elements are lost or their order is disturbed. The visible and tangible parts of our identity do not exist in a vacuum. They are grounded in our more widely lived reality, in the intricate and daedalian pattern of all constituting elements that this mosaic substrate lends to our lived experiences of the world: the sights, sounds, smells, touches, places, and other less tangible elements that infuse our sense of belonging, anywhere, any time.

The *tangible* elements of our identity and the *intangible* parts— the *mosaic substrate*—slot together in a unique way that creates a highly individualized fit, a pattern that gives us our special sense of being individuals. One's actual sense of identity is the product of the sum total of these two parts; it is the unique combination of the tangible and intangible, and it is this uniquely personal pattern that creates our sense of familiarity, relative stability, and continuity of being. It enables us to "read life," to experience ourselves and our surroundings with a degree of predictability.

I would argue that this unique fit creates what we could call "onto-ecological settledness." The term "onto-ecological" refers to the relationship between the totality of one's being and the totality of one's environment. Usually, terms that refer to the wholeness of a human being include only certain parts of this totality, e.g. body and mind, personal and social, conscious and unconscious, emotional and intellectual, external and internal. I have chosen terms that mean to address the entirety and completeness of both the person and his or her environment. The "ontology" of a person covers the fullness of one's being, existence, and becoming—and similarly, the term "ecology" covers all dimensions of all inhabited environments.

It is important to appreciate that this onto-ecological settledness is not an ideal state of an individuated, harmonious, and fulfilled personality. Instead, it is the settled arrangement and pattern, which, consisting of the unique mixture of positive and negative elements, creates a certain fluency of life, familiarity, stability, and predictability—regardless of how satisfactory or unsatisfactory this state may be. Ordinarily this settledness is not at all static, although it may appear to be so; instead, it is highly dynamic, always changing and adapting according to the changes in the person and the environment. The *bearable* changes occur within certain margins that enable the sustainment of our sense of continuity and stability. This change within margins is directly related to the sense of home, to the experience of being at home, of being contained by the inter-relationship of one's being and one's environment. However, when upheavals occur over and above a particular degree of intensity, our settledness gets disturbed in a felt way. The state that is then created I call "nostalgic disorientation."

Remember that the unique fit of both parts of our identity creates the onto-ecological settledness that maintains a stable sense of being. When upheaval destroys, dislocates, or reshuffles that particular fit, the unmistakable result is a sense of disorientation, discomfort, and distress that can best be described on the whole as *nostalgic* disorientation because it is not a known disorientation but one that activates a strong yearning for a return to the predictability of the familiar *settledness*. The nostalgic element is crucial and particular, chosen due to its specific Homeric connotations. "Nostalgic" is not used here in its usual modern denotation or dictionary definition, i.e. a "sentimental longing *for* or regretful memory of a period of the past." *Nostos* in Homeric Greek refers to the strong yearning to return home. But in combination with *algos* (pain), nostalgia conveys the acute pain, the intense and painful urge in the yearning for home, the ache involved in homesickness. Therefore, "nostalgic disorientation" is not just any ordinary disorientation, but the specific one that activates the longing, the thirst, the hunger for a return to the familiarity and comfort that the now disturbed onto-ecological settledness once provided.

When this type of disorientation emerges, a person experiences definitely and most markedly a mixture of rather intangible and difficult to identify types of discomfort. These include a sense of an inexplicable gap, a feeling of unreality, unsafety, unpredictability; lack of familiarity; lack of confidence; pervasive anxiety; and psychic ache and frozenness. It is important to clarify emphatically that these are not psychiatric symptoms as such, although extreme forms of unattended nostalgic disorientation may lead to psychiatric symptomatology. Thus, although nostalgic disorientation does not appear by convention as a psychiatric disorder, the felt discomfort and distress are so real that the debilitating effects should not be underestimated.

Ordinarily, we tend to appreciate only the distressing effects of identified pathological conditions, especially psychological ones or, even more so, psychiatric disorders. Yet, people who have involuntarily lost the sense of home, who have experienced a feeling of being dislocated, are most likely to experience the activation of some form of nostalgic disorientation whether or not they also suffer from any additional and specific psychological or psychiatric symptomatology.

Involuntarily dislocated persons are invariably capable of expressing their experiences of specific losses or changes with respect to the elements that contribute to their *tangible* identity, e.g. family members, material possessions, houses and land, jobs, positions, social roles, relationships, communities. They are aware of these losses and stand a good chance to grasp their condition. However, when their experience is not, "I lost this or that" but rather "I am lost," then it is more problematic because by definition the specific causes of nostalgic disorientation are nearly ungraspable.

It is now possible to see why this specific type of disorientation is more painful than the other familiar psychological conditions in these situations: (a) its causes are not visible although its effects are most felt and debilitating; (b) it triggers a powerful need to identify the causes, a need which often leads to deceptive results, to an over-concretized but specious aetiology that exacerbates the disorientation and the yearning for a solution; and (c) it activates a strong and painful yearning to re-establish the disturbed onto-ecological settledness of the lost home—but the problem is, which home? Past, present, or future? Geographical, cultural, or social, etc? Place of origin, or desired goal? Ideal, or real? Specific, or abstract? Concrete and static, or dynamic and changing? One, or many?

In desperate efforts to return to a specific and familiar feeling of being-at-home, and compelled by the nostalgic disorientation (that activates yearnings for reified homecomings), involuntarily dislocated people experience compounding confusion that further augments their disorientation. The entangled complexities—with their elusiveness and incomprehensibility—serve to engender additional pain, irritation, frustration, impatience, and anger.

It is of paramount importance to appreciate these complexities outside of the confines of traditional pathologizing approaches, and to acknowledge that the failures inherent in nostalgic disorientation can also contain most positive and, indeed, renewing potentials.

Regardless of the real external circumstances that bring about the reshuffling of the onto-ecological settledness and that, in turn, activate the nostalgic disorientation, it is always possible for the people concerned to put into constructive use all the powerful motivational force provided by both the *nostos* and *algos*. Thus they can embark on a committed search to reorganize the existing *status quo*, which could involve, for instance, a review and a re-evaluation of their aims and goals, contributing to refresh stagnant settledness, to dismantle and rejuvenate outdated life and home arrangements, and to develop more flexibility in a currently rigid, static, and sterile identity.

For this chance to be seized, we need to grasp the complexities of homecomings and identities and avoid focusing on negative epistemology that conceptualizes loss and failure as deficits or pathology. In this way, the failures brought on by nostalgic disorientation can be recognized as unique opportunities to expose the limits of an existing onto-ecological settledness and to inaugurate new awareness of these complexities. New awareness, in turn, can transform failure and disorientation into fuel for renewal that can activate new meanings, new identities and values, and novel and more appropriate forms of onto-ecological settledness.

Hence, the yearning for home can be diverted from the urge to return to an obsolete, destroyed, or deformed settledness, to the launching of a pursuit for new homes, for the creation of a more satisfactory and fulfilling existence and life meaning. In short, even the most catastrophic failures can fuel our efforts to re-position ourselves within our own onto-ecology. This is precisely the message of the Homeric *Odyssey*—homecoming is not just about returning home. It is also about recreating a new home within the context of an existing one, and about grasping and negotiating the complexities involved.

TRAUMA, RESILIENCE, AND ADVERSITY-ACTIVATED DEVELOPMENT

Now let us expand even further our conceptualization of failure. In discussion at the Jungian Odyssey conference, an eye surgeon told us that her professional practice cannot afford any margin for failure. She was absolutely right. A slight error by the surgeon and the patient can be blinded. Blinding somebody is a calamitous failure, indeed. There are no two ways about this; it is not a question of different perspectives, here. Undeniably, in this context one's loss of sight would represent an ultimate failure. Yet, who knows? By becoming blind, a person may be able to begin to see things he or she had never seen before. We have endless examples of people who, after experiencing terrible misfortune, discover new horizons opening up and then they consider the misfortune as a blessing. These examples are, by all means, rare exceptions. However, it all depends on the way we conceptualize the event and its consequences, the way we epistemologically grasp the phenomenon in its entirety and complexity.

Nobody can deny that blinding someone constitutes a catastrophic failure. At the same time, we also need to open ourselves up to the wider range of implications brought about by such terrible events and experiences. The *Odyssey* instructs us to hold onto *both* perspectives—the losses and gains, the returning back and going forward, returning to the familiar but also opening up and exploring new vistas and meanings. One of the *Odyssey's* key messages is to hold onto to these complexities and not to succumb to reified epistemologies that privilege exclusively one pole of meaning, invariably, the negative one.

In a similar vein, we should also understand the complexities involved in the context of psychological trauma. To begin with, nostalgic disorientation can easily be confused with psychological trauma; indeed, the most readily available framework to understand the incurred losses and distress is trauma. But what do we mean by "trauma"? The question is important because today the word "trauma" is used in diverse contexts that cover the widest possible spectrum, from the most debilitating psychiatric conditions to the most innocuous and trivial forms of discomfort. A cursory look at the daily newspapers in every country testifies to this astonishing array of meanings. Yet the idea persists that all of us understand precisely what one means by "trauma."

It is commonly known that trauma, a Greek word, means wound or injury and that it comes from the Greek verb, *titrosko*, meaning "to pierce." Hence the mark of being pierced or wounded is the injury, the trauma. My own etymological research shows that the origin of the verb "to pierce" (*titrosko*) in Greek is the verb *teiro*, "to rub," and in ancient Greek it had two meanings—to rub in and to rub off, to rub away.[13] When one rubs in something on one's skin, inevitably that will produce some piercing of the skin and, consequently, a wound. However, rubbing off or rubbing away has a completely different outcome. It would be to erase something, as one rubs off pencil writing on paper using a rubber or an eraser. Accordingly, a devastating experience may indeed break the skin, the protective membrane of our psychological system and cause a psychological injury (a "trauma"). But *at the same time*, it also has the power to erase previously held and maybe outdated or ill-adapted views and values. People who have suffered calamitous events will experience *in addition* to psychological injury a powerful sense of reviewing their entire lives. When (and if) we as psychologists or therapists create the space for their narratives and for our own listening, we will hear variations on this theme: "Because I came so close to death, now I see myself, my life, and life in general differently..." And they will add their own experience of this kind of change, for instance they value life more, they do not want to waste their life with inconsequential pursuits, etc.

Again, the emphasis here is on the need to grasp the complexity of appreciating *both* consequences of the devastating events. This is the true meaning of trauma, according to its original connotation. Yet again we note that, this is not the way we tend to approach the impact of catastrophic events; instead, the overwhelming inclination is to view all consequences in an exclusively negative way.

Over the years, I have developed an "adversity grid" to provide a framework that allows us to appreciate the wide range of responses, impacts, and consequences to exposures to adversity. The grid is now used in many contexts all over the world by humanitarian organizations, community workers, and clinicians, to obtain the wide range of implications after disastrous events—be they personal, communal, or of national scope in contexts of economic crisis, political or religious persecution, war, or natural disaster. The grid simply reminds us that there are least three different types of responses to adversity (Figure 5).

Levels	Negative Injury, Wound			Resilience	Positive Adversity-Activated Development ADD
	PD Psychiatric Disorders PTSD	DPR Distressful Psychological Reactions	OHS / ND Ordinary Human Suffering		
Individual					
Family					
Community					
Society / Culture					

Figure 5. *The Adversity Grid.*[12]

(a) *Negative responses* include at least three degrees of severity, i.e. psychiatric disorders (e.g. post-traumatic stress disorder), distressful psychological reactions and ordinary human suffering. This means that not all negative responses are "traumatic" in the same way. Although these are definitely negative responses and they are not pleasant, this does not mean that people necessarily require professional assistance (apart from the psychiatric disorders). Ordinarily, the overwhelming majority of people address these negative responses using existing meaning-creating forms that help them survive and move on with life.

(b) *Resilience*, i.e. positives qualities, characteristics, behaviors, functioning, relationships, all the strengths of a person (or of a family or of a community) that existed before the exposure to adversity and were retained after this exposure. This category is often neglected. In every situation, regardless of how difficult it may be, every person (and every family, every community) succeeds in retaining some of their strengths. However, under the emotional pressures of the pain and disorientation, the strengths are often neglected or even completely ignored. It is worth noting that the term "resilience," like "trauma," has an endless array of very confusing meanings; here, it is used specifically according to the definition that I have provided.

(c) *Adversity-activated Development* (AAD) corresponds to the rubbing off function of the trauma. If we approach phenomena of adversity from an epistemologically open perspective that enables us to grasp the complexities involved instead of wearing blinkers that force us to focus exclusively on the negative responses, we will always discern another category of responses—AAD. This category corresponds to the saying that exists (with variations) in so many languages and cultures: "Whatever does not kill you, will strengthen you." *In addition to* (not instead of) all other responses, every exposure to adversity enables a person to experience some gains that were activated by the very exposure to adversity. The experience of dealing with adversity can always introduce new positives that did not exist before. Therefore, *adversity-activated development* is understood as the specific development that brings about new strengths, new positive qualities, characteristics, behaviors, functioning, and relationships that did not exist prior to the exposure to adversity and were activated precisely by that very exposure.

It is this new development that Shakespeare extols when he writes about adversity being both "sweet" and also "sour," as we saw in the opening quotes to this paper. I would argue that just as Homer uses "earth" and "smoke" to delineate the range of meanings of home, Shakespeare also uses a pair of opposites to remind us that adversity can taste *both* sweet and sour *at the same time*.

Every exposure to adversity creates opposite, coexisting responses. In every situation, we can discern the three above-described responses occurring *simultaneously* (not sequentially, one after the other)—but only if, reminded by the framework that the adversity grid provides, we maintain our epistemological openness and appreciate the complexities involved in these phenomena.

CLOSING REFLECTIONS

The essential message that this paper conveys is in line, most perfectly, with the Jungian approach. Without using Jungian terminology as such, every point made here resonates strongly with the Jungian emphasis against reification, against a crude causal-reductive epistemology that focuses exclusively on the pathological effects of a psychological crisis that underestimates the constructive potentialities. Jung's acute sensibility for the complexity is characterized in the following quotes: "Our sins and errors and mistakes are necessary to us, otherwise we are deprived of the most precious incentives to development."[13] "[T]here is no illness that is not at the same time an unsuccessful attempt at cure."[14] "A psychology of neurosis that sees only the negative elements empties out the baby with the bath water ..."[15]

Failure has been the overarching theme of this paper. Home, loss of home, and yearning for home are powerful realities and images that give central meaning to our lives. *Nostalgic disorientation* is a specific form of failure that aims to maintain a satisfactory *onto-ecological settledness*. Exposure to adversity often results in disorientation, in an unsettledness that is usually understood as "trauma." The widely accepted "trauma discourse" (i.e. the privileging of negative responses to adversity) constitutes our own failure to grasp the epistemological complexity of the archetypal dialectic "failure/success."

Failure, home, and trauma are the three crucibles within which the churning of our meaning of life is taking place. All three are central motifs that challenge us to transcend our existing context and refresh our perspectives. All three can potentially initiate substantial transformations in and around us if we succeed to discern their potentialities. Involuntary loss of intimate space and other, related calamitous situations represent instances of failure that can result in catastrophic outcomes. However, this only occurs if we fail to discern the opportunity that they can also provide for us. All these three can be considered as offering what satellite navigation devices do whenever their initially planned direction is changed: they flash the message "recalculating route," informing us that the change in direction is not catastrophic but it takes time to introduce the new adjustments. What is then required of us is patience and reflection in order to allow the new direction to emerge. *Nostalgic disorientation* and trauma can be appreciated as performing such "recalculating" operations, enabling us to devise new routes.

NOTES

¹ The research presented at the Jungian Odyssey and now in this article has been widely published and applied elsewhere. See for example, Renos K. Papadopoulos, "Refugees, Trauma, and Adversity-Activated Development," in *European Journal of Psychotherapy and Counseling*, 9(3), September 2007; "Refugees, Home and Trauma," in *Therapeutic Care for Refugees: No Place Like Home*, ed. Renos K. Papadopoulos, Tavistock Clinical Series (London: Karnac, 2002); "Political Violence, Trauma and Mental Health Interventions," in *Art Therapy and Political Violence, With Art, Without Illusion*, eds. Debra Kalmanowitz, Bobby Lloyd (London: Brunner-Routledge, 2005); "Extending Jungian Psychology, Working with Survivors of Political Upheavals," in *Sacral Revolutions, Reflecting on the Cutting Work of Andrew Samuels*, ed. Gottfried Heuer (London: Routledge, 2010); "The Umwelt and Networks of Archetypal Images: A Jungian Approach to Therapeutic Encounters in Humanitarian Contexts," in *Psychotherapy and Politics International,* Vol. 9, Number 3, 2009. Eds. note: For an excellent source that compiles the references and is available online, see Papadopoulos, *Enhancing Vulnerable Asylum Seekers' Protection (EVASP), Trainers' Handbook* (Rome: International Organization for Migration, [undated]), download from *International Organization for Migration, Psychosocial and Cultural Integration Unit*, "EVASP Handbook," www.evasp.eu (accessed April 1, 2015).

² Source Title, "A Ulysses Mosaic," uploaded to Flickr by Dennis Jarvis, reproduced according to the Creative Commons Attribution-Share Alike Generic license, at http://commons.wikimedia.org/wiki/File:Tunisia-4727_-_Ulysses.jpg (accessed September 4, 2014).

³ C.P. Cavafy, "Ithaca," in *Collected Poems*, trans. Edmund Keeley and Phillip Sherrard, ed. George Savidis, Rev. Ed. (Princeton, NJ: Princeton University Press, 1992), my italics.

⁴ Michael Wolgemut, Wilhelm Pleydenwurff, "Fenix Auis Vnica," in Schedel Hartmann, *Liber Chronicrum*, BSB Shelfmark: Rar. 287, viewable online at *World Digital Library*, the complete work at: http:/

/www.wdl.org/en/item/4108/ and "Fenix ..." at, http://www.wdl.org/en/item/4108/view/1/280/ (accessed September 4, 2014).

⁵ Charley Mason, Joey Patulka, Ali Zuckowski, Julian Maas, "Rise Like a Phoenix," first released by Conchita Wurst, May 10, 2014. For the complete lyrics see, http://www.eurovision.tv/event/lyrics?event=1873&song=31403 (accessed May 14, 2014).

⁶ Donald W. Winnicott, "Transitional Objects and Transitional Phenomena: A Study of the First Not-Me Possession," in *International Journal of Psychoanalysis*, 1953, 34(2), pp. 89-97.

⁷ Tanya Byron in Graeme Paton, Education Editor, "Children 'no longer allowed to fail,' Tanya Byron warns," *The Telegraph*, December 5, 2012, my italics. See http://www.telegraph.co.uk/education/educationnews/9725022/Children-no-longer-allowed-to-fail-Tanya-Byron-warns.html (accessed May 14, 2014).

⁸ Homer, *The Odyssey*, trans. E.V. Rieu [1942], cited in Papadopoulos, "Introduction," in *Therapeutic Care for Refugees*, p. 13, my italics.

⁹ John Hill, *At Home in the World, Sounds and Symmetries of Belonging*, Zurich Lecture Series in Analytical Psychology (New Orleans: Spring Journal Books, 2010).

¹⁰ T.S. Eliot, "Little Gidding," 1942, Number 4 of *Four Quartets* (NY: Harcourt Books, Harcourt Inc., 1943/1971), p. 59.

¹¹ Papadopoulos, "Refugees, Home and Trauma," in *Therapeutic Care for Refugees: No Place Like Home*.

¹² "The Adversity Grid," adapted from Papadopoulos, "The Trauma Grid," *Enhancing Vulnerable Asylum Seekers' Protection*, p. 22.

¹³ C.G. Jung, "Lecture Four, Discussion," *Analytical Psychology*, from the Tavistock Lectures delivered in English, 1935, Routledge Classics Edition (New York: Routledge, 1976/2014), p. 107.

¹⁴ C.G. Jung, "In Memory of Sigmund Freud [1939]," in "The Spirit in Man, Art, and Literature," *The Collected Works of C.G. Jung*, Vol. 15, eds. Sir Herbert Read, Michael Fordham, Gerhard Adler, William McGuire, trans. R.F.C. Hull, Bollingen Series XX, Fourth Printing (Princeton: Princeton University Press, 1978), § 68, hereinafter referenced as "CW", followed by the volume number and paragraph number.

¹⁵ C.G. Jung, "The State of Psychotherapy Today [1934]," CW 10, § 355.

3

Letting Go
of Success

Andrew Fellows

INTRODUCTION

The relationship between failure and success is not as straightforward as it seems at first glance. Letting go of success is sometimes the only way to avoid, or at least mitigate, failure. We will explore this paradox with individual and collective examples, and try to understand it from Jungian, classical, and mathematical perspectives, but let's begin with common sense.

What exactly is success? Suspecting that rather a lot of people believed they knew the answer, I searched the books section of Amazon, and came up with 188,124 hits for "success"—unsurprisingly more than eight times more than for "failure." Perched atop this enormous pile is *The Success Principles: How to Get from Where You Are to Where You Want to Be*, which claims that, "All you have to do is decide what it is you want, believe you deserve it, and practice the principles in this book, and success is yours."[1] Naturally the book trumpets its own success with glittering testimonials, such as, "If your goal is greater accomplishment, more money, more free time, and less stress, read and apply the proven principles in this book."[2]

Dictionaries define success as "the accomplishment of an aim or purpose" and "the attainment of fame, wealth, or social status," while its etymology is traced to "result, outcome," from the Latin *successus*, and "an advance, succession, happy outcome," from *succedere*, "come after" (succeed). The meaning "accomplishment of desired end" was first recorded in the 1580s. The *Online Etymology Dictionary* then unexpectedly proffers the following acerbic quotation from one of Jung's early associates:

> The moral flabbiness born of the bitch-goddess SUCCESS.
> That—with the squalid interpretation put on the word
> success—is our national disease.[3]

So ambivalence about success is nothing new (nor, apparently, is appalling misogyny). While it's easy to mock the popular notion of success, we must recognize its pervasive influence in the Zeitgeist, and especially in our individual and collective loss of soul.

Success and ambition are intimately related. Ambition is a particularly perplexing form of desire, not least because its results can range from the pinnacle of creative achievement to the abyss of destructive fixation. Clinging, or attachment, to desire, including the desire to become something, such as seeking wealth or fame, is identified as the origin of suffering in the Twelve Insights into the Four Noble Truths of Buddhism. To let go of success, this clinging must end. Perhaps the simplest and most robust generalization that we can make about ambition is that it is invariably a construct of the ego that sets some kind of goal as the criterion of success. We can divide these goals into two classes, which, in the language of mathematics, are "discrete" (separate) and "continuous."

To want to pass an exam, win a game, or climb a mountain are all examples of the ego setting discrete goals. Pass or fail, win or lose, summit or not, success or failure are clearly defined by these goals, and ambition is equally clearly resolved. Or are they? Am I satisfied with my performance in that exam or that game, irrespective of the result? Speaking as a lifelong mountaineer, I may want to reach the summit, but my fundamental criterion of success is getting off the hill safely, not getting to the top. Responsible climbing demands mental, as well as physical, balance, especially the ability to let go of an earlier goal, however cherished.

Ambition measured against continuous goals, which we sometimes call ideals, is inherently more problematic. The goals in that testimonial—"greater accomplishment, more money, more free time, and less stress"—are all examples. To ask, "How much is enough?" seldom elicits a benchmark for success, whereas failure is immediately apparent as "not enough." Therefore such ambition can be insatiable. To complicate matters further, ambition often manifests as continuous craving for discrete successes. Alfred Alvarez, for example, acknowledged this in the title of his biography of his friend and climbing partner, Mo Anthoine: *Feeding the Rat.* Each climb ends, but there is always a harder one.

In the worst case, both failure *and* success can lead to obsessive ambition and compulsive action. "If at first you don't succeed, try, try, and try again," could be complemented by, "If and when you do succeed, triumph, triumph, and triumph again." Either can spur us on to excellence; either can ensnare us in mindless fixation. The deciding factor is whether we cling or let go; the Buddhists were right.

We now turn from this rather *logical* look at success to an essentially *psycho*logical insight that has been systematically ignored for millennia. This is the inconvenient, and thoroughly unpopular, truth that too much success risks something altogether more dangerous, which the ancient Greeks called hubris.

Dynamics

Hubris is intoxication with success, extreme pride, or self-confidence, a loss of contact with reality and an overestimation of one's own competence, accomplishments or capabilities, which results in fatal retribution, or nemesis. In classical Greece, hubris described the actions of those who challenged the gods or their laws, especially in Greek tragedy, leading to the protagonist's downfall. It was considered the greatest sin of the ancient Greek world. In its modern usage too, hubris denotes overconfident pride and arrogance, which is characterized by a lack of humility. It is also referred to as "pride that blinds" because it often manifests as behavior that defies common sense. Hubris, the proverbial "pride before the fall," can manifest in both individual and collective attitudes and behavior.

But why must nemesis follow hubris? Is it because there is only one way to go from the top, and that is down? This popular explanation is superficial and often disingenuous. It may be literally true of a mountain, but what of continuous goals, endless ambition, and prolonged success? For a deeper understanding we must enter the realm of Jungian psychology to consider *enantiodromia*. Jung acknowledged the origin of this term in the philosophy of Heraclitus as "the play of opposites in the course of events, the view that everything that exists turns into its opposite."[4] However he coined the term himself:

> I use the term enantiodromia for the emergence of the unconscious opposite in the course of time. This characteristic phenomenon practically always occurs when an extreme, one-sided tendency dominates conscious life; in time an equally powerful counterposition is built up, which first inhibits the conscious performance and subsequently breaks through the conscious control.[5]

Enantiodromia is a cornerstone of Jungian psychology, which has therefore sometimes been called "the psychology of opposites." It is also an integral aspect of classical Eastern world views, most well known in the West as the endless interplay of Yin and Yang:

> The Chinese world view is essentially dynamic and cyclical: all things constantly change, the only permanent reality is change. Thus Yin and Yang are not static categories. They are animated by a cyclical movement, which transforms them into each other... When the light quality (Yang) reaches its culmination, it gives birth to the seed of the dark quality (Yin), which at that moment begins to grow. When the dark quality (Yin) reaches its apex, it develops inside itself the seed of the light quality, which at that moment begins to grow.[6]

What does this mean in practice? Is it always as smooth as the contours of the *taijitu*, which has acquired iconic status within the New Age movement? Of course not, as the Chinese themselves have known for millennia. The *Eranos I Ching* introduction notes that the essential word in the book's title is *yi* (易) which means, among other things, "change." However, this *yi* isn't the regular change involved in the cycle of day and night or the natural growth of living things, but unpredictable change. There is a vivid description of it in another of the Five Classics of ancient Chinese literature:

> When in years, months and days the season has no *yi*, the
> hundred cereals ripen, the administration is enlightened, talented
> men of the people are distinguished, the house is peaceful and
> at ease. When in days, months and years the season has *yi*, the
> hundred cereals do not ripen, the administration is dark and
> unenlightened, talented men of the people are in petty positions,
> the house is not at peace.[7]

This sounds uncomfortably like the times we live in:

> We have *yi* when things are off track, when chaos irrupts into
> our life and the usual bearings no longer suffice for orientation.
> We all know that such times can be very fertile—and extremely
> painful, disconcerting and full of anxiety.[8]

Mathematicians have been aware of unpredictable change for
centuries, but only in recent decades had sufficient computing power
to explore these regions of behavior in nonlinear systems. It is sweetly
ironic, given the topic of this lecture, that it was the *failure* of Edward
Lorentz's weather-modeling computer to deliver reproducible results
in 1961 (the year of Jung's death) that triggered the *success* of chaos
theory. Surely Jung, ever the polymath, would have been as engaged
with the new sciences of chaos theory, complexity, and emergence as
he was with those of his day. Nonlinear systems can exhibit wildly
variable sensitivity to perturbations—Lorentz's "butterfly effect" being
at the high extreme—and abrupt transitions from one state to another
at so-called "tipping points." Such behavior manifests in both nature
and human nature, from the formation of a hurricane to the
constellation of a complex. Life consists of both predictable and
unpredictable change:

> Life itself arises at the boundary between order and chaos: it
> requires both, it is a daughter of both. On the side of perfect
> order there is only dead stability, inertia, symmetry,
> thermodynamic equilibrium. Nothing very interesting can
> happen there: everything is too predictable, it resembles death
> more than life. But the side of total disorder is not very interesting
> either: forms appear and disappear too quickly, there is a total
> lack of symmetry, everything is too unpredictable. It is on the
> edge between order and chaos that the subtle dance of life takes
> place: here the real complexities arise, here forms bend and loop
> and transmute and evolve.[9]

Returning to Jung's description of enantiodromia, we can see that it often manifests as unpredictable change, *yi*, with all its consequences; likewise nemesis, otherwise we could avoid it. We will now explore the individual and collective implications of these dynamics for letting go of success.

STAGES OF LIFE

The framework *par excellence* for such exploration is Jung's 1931 essay, "The Stages of Life," which he describes as his contribution to answering the unavoidable, basic question, "Why does man, in obvious contrast to the animal world, have problems at all?"[10] John-Raphael Staude, in his book *The Adult Development of C. G. Jung*, notes that:

> The implications of Jung's psychology for life-span developmental psychology are profound. Instead of focusing on the achievement of ego competencies, Jung evaluated lives in terms of their balance, well-roundedness, wholeness. He emphasized developing the underdeveloped aspects of the self and maintaining an ongoing dialogue between the ego and non-ego aspects of the self as a total self-regulating developing system. Jung's theory offers a compensatory view to the ego psychology dominating life-span developmental psychology today.[11]

Starting from Jung's analogy with the course of the sun, we will focus on the mid-life transition. Jung writes:

> ... the basic cause of all the difficulties of this transition is to be found in a deep-seated and peculiar change within the psyche. In order to characterize it I must take for comparison the daily course of the sun,—but a sun that is endowed with human feeling and man's limited consciousness. In the morning it rises from the nocturnal sea of unconsciousness and looks upon the wide, bright world which lies before it in an expanse that steadily widens the higher it climbs in the firmament.[12]

So far, so good, but now enantiodromia upsets everything:

> At the stroke of noon the descent begins. And the descent means the reversal of all the ideals and values that were cherished in the morning. The sun falls into contradiction with itself.[13]

Naturally we resist—who wants to reverse their ideals and values?

> The nearer we approach to the middle of life, and the better we
> have succeeded in entrenching ourselves in our personal attitudes
> and social positions, the more it appears as if we had discovered
> the right course and the right ideals and principles of behavior.
> For this reason we suppose them to be eternally valid, and make
> a virtue of unchangeably clinging to them.... Many—far too
> many—aspects of life which should also have been experienced
> lie in the lumber-room among dusty memories; but sometimes,
> too, they are glowing coals under grey ashes.[14]

Our ego may cling to success, but some of the "glowing coals" in the
unconscious threaten to turn transition into crisis.

> Statistics show a rise in the frequency of mental depressions in
> men about forty. In women the neurotic difficulties generally
> begin somewhat earlier. We see that in this phase of life—
> between thirty-five and forty—an important change in the
> human psyche is in preparation. At first it is not a conscious and
> striking change; it is rather a matter of indirect signs of a change
> which seems to take its rise in the unconscious. Often it is
> something like a slow change in a person's character; in another
> case certain traits may come to light which had disappeared since
> childhood; or again, one's previous inclinations and interests
> begin to weaken and others take their place.[15]

Remember Jung's definition of enantiodromia—"an equally
powerful counterposition is built up, which first inhibits the conscious
performance." Although such neuroses manifest in different ways, there
is a general sense of losing certainty and increasing self-doubt, of
running out of steam. Either libido enters limbo, or:

> Conversely—and this happens very frequently—one's
> cherished convictions and principles, especially the moral ones,
> begin to harden and to grow increasingly rigid until, somewhere
> around the age of fifty, a period of intolerance and fanaticism is
> reached. It is as if the existence of these principles were
> endangered and it were therefore necessary to emphasize them
> all the more.[16]

Jung views such clinging to success as failure, for he asserts
unequivocally that enantiodromia, "the emergence of the unconscious

opposite in the course of time," which means letting go of success, is not only inevitable, it is part of life's great plan:

> A human being would certainly not grow to be seventy or eighty years old if this longevity had no meaning for the species. The afternoon of human life must also have a significance of its own and cannot be merely a pitiful appendage to life's morning. The significance of the morning undoubtedly lies in the development of the individual, our entrenchment in the outer world, the propagation of our kind, and the care of our children. This is the obvious purpose of nature. But when this purpose has been attained—and more than attained—shall the earning of money, the extension of conquests, and the expansion of life go steadily on beyond the bounds of all reason and sense? Whoever carries over into the afternoon the law of the morning, or the natural aim, must pay for it with damage to his soul…[17]

Joseph Campbell once memorably described mid-life crisis as what happens when you climb to the top of the ladder—and discover it's against the wrong wall! Dante's *Divine Comedy* begins with a succinct exposition of the feeling of disorientation, and the imminent confrontation with the unconscious, characteristic of the mid-life transition:

> Midway upon the journey of our life
> I found myself within a forest dark,
> For the straightforward pathway had been lost.[18]

Later we learn that Dante's character has his thirty-fifth birthday during the second stage of his epic journey through Inferno and Purgatorio to Paradiso.

The phenomenon that Jung so acutely described is nothing new, nor was he merely theorizing from a safe distance. Jung let go of success during his own "confrontation with the unconscious" in mid-life. He broke with Freud and the psychoanalytical group, embarked upon the Red Book, and endured years of introspective personal crisis and professional isolation, the purpose of which only became fully apparent decades later:

> The years, of which I have spoken to you, when I pursued the inner images, were the most important time of my life. Everything else is to be derived from this. It began at that time, and the later details hardly matter anymore. My entire life

consisted in elaborating what had burst forth from the
unconscious and flooded me like an enigmatic stream and
threatened to break me. That was the stuff and material for
more than only one life. Everything later was merely the outer
classification, the scientific elaboration, and the integration
into life. But the numinous beginning, which contained
everything, was then.[19]

So much for Dante and Jung, but what about us lesser mortals?

INDIVIDUAL CASE

I have experienced the mid-life transition in myself, and in my
practice. It can be a deeply distressing process, in which the ego is in
conflict with the slow but inexorable dynamics of the psyche as a whole.
This is dramatically illustrated by a dream of one of my analysands,
which I present with his permission.

"Bill" was a forty-three-year-old high-flyer in transatlantic finance,
a wealthy and successful family man. His presenting complaints were
loss of motivation, problems getting up and falling asleep, withdrawal
from social activities, and feeling trapped between work and home life.
In other words, he suffered from precisely the "inhibition of conscious
performance" that Jung had described in enantiodromia and mid-life.
Bill summed this up as, "I need time for myself." It was a striking
contrast to his "work hard, play hard" ethos. Bill's fear of losing his
job was at an existential level, as "loser of the universe." He worried
about how others would view him, and about being dependent on
help. His need for time alone became so acute that about twice a week
he stopped in a café on his way home from work, then felt guilty about
doing so. Bill had said that he always tried to be the center of attention
and was competitive, but also a team player, so I suggested that his
café stops might be the start of an opposing tendency, that his libido
was turning inward. In the fifth session Bill presented, after much
hesitation, the following dream. He was so upset by it, and ashamed
of it, that he had waited two weeks to disclose it, and he took another
month to write it down:

> I'm in an unfamiliar town on a weekday evening at dusk,
> sneaking through a park to a large soccer stadium. I hear
> the crowd inside since the game is already on. I remember
> that I had seen somebody blowing something up by

spraying gasoline all over the place, and igniting it by dragging a steel bar (like those you find on construction sites) along the concrete floor to make sparks. I am not sure whether I saw this on TV or in 'real' life, but I decide to do exactly the same thing. I did not really plan this, and I do not know where I got the gasoline and the metal pole from. But now I spray the gasoline at the wall and drag the pole, the sparks ignite the gasoline, and I blow up part of the stadium. I do not turn around and run away, but continue walking past the stadium, and can see from a distance the disaster I created. I see ambulances coming to the aid of the dead and wounded. I evade attention and walk home. I have no remorse for what I've done, just an increasing fear of being caught. At home I feel that the police are closing in, and start to prepare an alibi. It was a copycat crime—I had briefly seen a man my age wearing a black balaclava do exactly the same thing. I get even more afraid, not necessarily because I will have to go to jail, but rather that I will have to admit what a horrible thing I did and everybody will know what a bad person I am. The fear gets so bad that I wake up, my heart is pumping fast…

Clearly this was a shadow encounter, as were most of Bill's dreams, but one in which he emulated rather than opposed his shadow. The image is explosive because Bill's conscious bond to the collective was so strong, just like the mass identification of football fans with their teams in a stadium. Both the dream ego and the shadow were attacking three of Bill's most cherished ideals and goals—to be competitive, to be conventional (a team player is also a team supporter), and yet to be the center of attention. What is remarkable is that he felt so ashamed *about* the dream but not *in* the dream. In waking life Bill was shocked, and frightened that he might be a terrorist, but in the dream he calmly planned how to evade the authoritarian aspect of the collective, and perhaps also of his personal father complex. His radical act of destruction even used an element of construction—the steel bar— and unleashed tremendous energy. For something new to be born, something has to die.

Bill eventually left analysis, still blocked by his literalism from the symbolic awareness needed for transformation. The powerful and threatening imagery from his unconscious petrified him. Deeply wedded to convention, his ego had too much invested in "business as usual" to let go of success, to leap into the unknown. Bill didn't get beyond those first three lines of Dante, he failed to find his *anima* Beatrice, and I failed to be his Virgil. In the language of nonlinear dynamics, Bill's psyche was in a state of low sensitivity to perturbations.

That was five years ago, and I wonder how the tug-of-war between ego and Self has developed since then, for the "glowing coals" in Bill's unconscious were already hot enough to start a fire. Everything has its time. This is the ancient Greek notion of *kairos*, meaning the right or opportune moment, awareness of which is as important in the practice room as it is in the world at large, to which we finally turn.

COLLECTIVE ISSUES

Could we apply Jung's "Stages of Life" model to situate modern civilization in our development as a species? Both Freud and Jung speculated that the psychology of the individual could be extrapolated to the collective. In the language of nonlinear systems, this is called "self-similarity across scale." In 1930, Sigmund Freud wrote:

> If the development of civilization has such a far-reaching similarity to the development of the individual and if it employs the same methods, may we not be justified in reaching the diagnosis that, under the influence of cultural urges, some civilizations, or some epochs of civilization—possibly the whole of mankind—have become "neurotic"?[20]

Jung, introducing his theories to a wider audience, wrote:

> If, for a moment, we regard mankind as one individual, we see that the human race is like a person carried away by unconscious powers.[21]

So what might such an extrapolation reveal in the world view of our civilization, especially the industrialized West that is driving globalization? What could it teach our species about letting go of success?

In technological and numerical terms, human development has been extraordinarily successful. We permanently inhabit every continent and, with a population of over seven billion, are by far the most numerous large mammals. The agricultural and industrial revolutions have accelerated food production and resource extraction, offering us unprecedented security, comfort, and longevity despite our growing numbers. Until very recently no end to our success was in sight, there were no limits to growth. But how many great civilizations of the past had the same belief? Consider, for example Edward Gibbon's analysis of the Roman Empire:

> The decline of Rome was the natural and inevitable effect of immoderate greatness. Prosperity ripened the principle of decay; the causes of destruction multiplied with the extent of conquest; and as soon as time or accident had removed the artificial supports, the stupendous fabric yielded to the pressure of its own weight.[22]

By "immoderate greatness" Gibbon meant, of course, hubris. William Ophuls, an independent scholar who is well acquainted with Jungian psychology, elaborates this theme with unflinching clarity in his eponymous book:

> A civilization's very magnitude conspires against it to cause downfall. Civilizations are hard-wired for self-destruction. They travel an arc from initial success to terminal decay and ultimate collapse due to intrinsic biophysical limits combined with an inexorable trend toward moral decay and practical failure.

> Because our own civilization is global, its collapse will also be global, as well as uniquely devastating owing to the immensity of its population, complexity and consumption. To avoid the common fate of all past civilizations will require a radical change in our ethos—to wit, the deliberate renunciation of greatness— lest we precipitate a dark age in which the arts and adornments of civilization are partially or completely lost.[23]

The arc of civilizations graphically parallels Jung's "Stages of Life" and the deliberate renunciation of greatness requires letting go of success. But just as in Bill's individual case, a tug-of-war has begun in the correspondingly petrified collective. A widening gulf is emerging between adherents to "business as usual" and those demanding the radical change in our ethos identified by Ophuls. This increasingly dangerous split crosses national boundaries and outmoded left/right political divides, but is habitually projected onto them. Fritjof Capra hit the nail on the head with this trenchant observation:

> One of the most difficult things for people in our culture to understand is the fact that if you do something that is good, then more of the same will not necessarily be better. This, to me, is the essence of ecological thinking.[24]

… and the essence of letting go of success. For its antithesis, consider what Rex Tillerson, CEO of ExxonMobil, said about climate change to the U.S. Council on Foreign Relations three decades later:

> We have spent our entire existence adapting, okay? So we will adapt to this. Changes to weather patterns that move crop production areas around—we'll adapt to that. It's an engineering problem, and it has engineering solutions.[25]

Tillerson wants everyone else to adapt, so that his transnational behemoth, which coincidentally has enormous engineering resources, doesn't need to. There is, understandably, massive inertia in our immense civilization, but also disturbing evidence of "cherished convictions and principles beginning to harden and to grow increasingly rigid," as described by Jung and exemplified by Bill. Appropriately enough, the epicenter of this petrification is now the fossil fuel industry which, adopting the tactics and advocates of big tobacco, now employs political manipulation and public disinformation more than any other corporate sector to promote its commercial interests over environmental realities.

Jung, who lived through two World Wars, was profoundly concerned with the collective dangers of his time, especially the Cold War and the threat of nuclear annihilation towards the end of his life. His fears may be summed up in his bleak warning that, "… the world today hangs by a thin thread, and that thread is the psyche of man."[26]

Collective dangers are *not* an engineering problem, for it is psyche that invents and wields the tool. The dangers that concerned Jung are now compounded by environmental perils that he could never have foreseen. A year after Jung's death, the American marine biologist Rachel Carson's wake-up call, *Silent Spring*, was published. Her analysis of the impacts of artificial pesticides exposed mass deception motivated by industrial profit, inspired a grassroots environmental movement, and led to the creation of the U.S. Environmental Protection Agency. Meanwhile President Kennedy's environmental advisor, the economist Kenneth Boulding, observed that, "'Anyone who believes in indefinite growth in anything physical, on a physically finite planet, ... is either mad—or an economist.'"[27]

Hardly rocket science, yet half a century later economic growth remains the holy grail of our age, despite being the principal driver of our most harmful impacts. We have the science to understand these impacts, and the resources and technology to minimize them, but the action that reason dictates is thwarted by psychological factors— hubris, greed, selfishness, peer pressure, complacency, and so on. Thus Jung's challenge to our excessive faith in reason and, more generally, our "monotheism of consciousness" is as relevant as ever, but it has also contributed to his widespread rejection; otherness is unpopular, and what greater other *is* there than the irrational unconscious? Wouter Hanegraaff summarizes the otherness and rejection of Jung:

> He took the basic idea ... of a history of the magical "nightside of nature" and its experiential manifestations, but repackaged it in modern psychological terms as the history of Western culture's suppressed unconscious.... In this narrative, the official representatives of the mainstream (Christian theologians, rational philosophers, modern scientists) have always tried to suppress it...[28]

Back *in* the mainstream, contemporary Western hubris arguably reached its apogee in *The End of History* by the Stanford political scientist Francis Fukuyama, which is tantamount to a reformulated Manifest Destiny for our time:

> What we may be witnessing is not just the end of the Cold War, or the passing of a particular period of post-war history, but the end of history as such: that is, the end point of mankind's ideological evolution and the universalization of Western liberal democracy as the final form of human government.[29]

Flattery gets you everywhere, and Fukuyama's triumphalist fundamentalism has mesmerized Western policymakers and petrified our social imagination. This is precisely the "period of intolerance and fanaticism" that Jung warned against in individual development. Thus the unprecedented state surveillance, corporate infiltration, and media brainwashing that desperately seek to preserve Fukuyama's ideal by excluding otherness have, in reality, perverted democracy into consenting oligarchy. I should emphasize here that the otherness of Jungian psychology, and the *complexio oppositorum* itself, transcend mere politics, and are thus non-aligned.

Marie-Louise von Franz warned that the shadow of Jungian psychology is inflation, so we should heed Alfred Korzybski's famous caveat that "the map is not the territory."[30] Jung was the first to admit that his analytical psychology, for all its richness, is essentially a map of largely unknown and unknowable territory. The convergence of Eastern and Western classical thinking, modern mathematics, and Jungian insights I present is arguably as much an indication of the incompleteness of each as it is a mutual endorsement. Moreover, I have simplified and selected from each to make my case; reality is of course more nuanced and differentiated.

Nonetheless, Jung's importance for Ophuls' "deliberate renunciation of greatness," ending hubris, and letting go of success goes far beyond otherness merely as opposition. Thanks to the broad historical sweep of his synthesis, and his due recognition of the slow-moving unconscious, Jung naturally embraced the long term view that is so conspicuously absent from mainstream consciousness. In *Aion*, he envisions the passing from one astrological age to the next due to the precession of the equinoxes, an event that occurs approximately every 2160 years, as a deep and unsettling transition in the collective. This corresponds with a major life transition in an individual; "as above, so below," or self-similarity across scale—choose your map and language. Although there is no consensus on a precise date, we are undoubtedly in a period of transition from the astrological age of Pisces into that of Aquarius, about which Jung writes:

> If, as seems probable, the aeon of the fishes is ruled by the archetypal motif of the hostile brothers, then the approach of the next Platonic month, namely Aquarius, will constellate the problem of the union of opposites. It will then no longer be possible to write off evil as the mere privation of good; its real existence will have to be recognized. This problem can be solved neither by philosophy, nor by economics, nor by politics, but only by the individual human being, via his experience of the living spirit…[31]

Jung completes the circle from the collective back to the individual, and his bleak prognosis sends a mixed message to the New Age movement. Individuation is not a wellness course, and the journey towards balance and wholeness by integrating the neglected and rejected aspects of the personality is uncomfortable and psychologically difficult. But taking the first step, which is just admitting even the existence of otherness, and thereby accepting that our world view is limited, isn't intellectually demanding. Even Homer Simpson manages it in his simple confession that, "Every time I learn something new, it pushes the old stuff out of my brain"! Behind the humor is a touching and sincere humility—the most direct antidote to hubris, for they cannot coexist. Jung, ever mindful of such limitations, reminded us that,

> Science comes to a stop at the frontiers of logic, but nature does
> not—she thrives on ground as yet untrodden by theory.[32]

Our leaders, our civilization, our species, our consciousness—*we* cling tenaciously to past success, ignoring overwhelming evidence that we must now let go of it. But opposition is growing within, just like Jung's unconscious counter-position; the hostile brothers are now constellated on a global scale, with terrifying implications. But where exactly are we in this, the biggest enantiodromia of them all? Jung, informed by astrology as we have seen, clearly believed we are at the turning point:

> We are living in what the Greeks called the kairos—the right
> moment—for a "metamorphosis of the gods," of the
> fundamental principles and symbols.... Coming generations
> will have to take account of this momentous transformation
> if humanity is not to destroy itself through the might of its
> own technology and science.[33]

So what are we to actually do? As Jung repeatedly emphasized, each of us must find her or his own way. I earnestly hope, however, that we can all be inspired and motivated by these words from the ground-breaking author of *Small is Beautiful*:

> Can we rely on it that a "turning around" will be accomplished
> by enough people quickly enough to save the modern world?
> This question is often asked, but no matter what the answer, it

will mislead. The answer "Yes" would lead to complacency, the
answer "No" to despair. It is desirable to leave these perplexities
behind us and get down to work.[34]

This means both inner work *and* outer action, for individuation is
worthless unless brought back into the outer world. As von Franz
said, to reach that point where outer and inner reality become one
is the goal of individuation. Recognizing the *unus mundus* in theory
obliges us to attend very carefully to our social and environmental
impacts in practice.

Our success as a species has unleashed natural forces that guarantee
us a rough ride for decades, perhaps centuries, to come. We will need
courage and strength, not only to endure this, but also to deliberately
renounce our greatness, to let go of success. Perhaps here we should
recall these remorsefully impassioned words of Edward Whymper, to
whose memory I tip my climbing helmet in this magnificent alpine
setting here at Grindelwald:

> Climb if you will, but remember that courage and strength are
> nought without prudence, and that a momentary negligence
> may destroy the happiness of a lifetime. Do nothing in haste;
> look well to each step; and from the beginning think what may
> be the end.[35]

My friend Jeff Kiehl, who is both a Jungian analyst and a climate
scientist at the National Centre for Atmospheric Research in Colorado,
has observed that the feelings about climate change experienced by
his lecture audiences—denial, helplessness, anger, and so on—are all
characteristic of trauma. So I want to conclude with a reminder that
the crisis we are in has a *purpose*, that collectively as well as individually
we can take heart from Jung's assertion that, "the afternoon of human
life must also have a significance of its own and cannot be merely a
pitiful appendage to life's morning."

NOTES

[1] Jack Canfield, *The Success Principles: How to Get from Where You
Are to Where You Want to Be* (William Morrow Paperbacks; Reprint
edition, 2006), p. xxix.

[2] *Ibid.* (Front Matter, un-numbered page).

[3] William James to H.G. Wells, Sept. 11, 1906, cited in "success (n.)," in Douglas Harper, *Online Etymological Dictionary*, © 2010-2014, at www.etymonline.com (accessed May 1, 2014).

[4] C.G. Jung, "Definitions" [1921], in *Psychological Types, The Collected Works of C.G. Jung*, eds. Sir Herbert Read, Michael Fordham, Gerhard Adler, William McGuire, trans. R.F.C. Hull, Bollingen Series XX (Princeton, NJ: Princeton University Press, 1971), Vol. 6, § 708. All future references to Jung's *Collected Works*, abbreviated to CW, will be with chapter titles followed by the original publication dates, volume, and paragraph numbers.

[5] *Ibid.*, "Definitions," CW 6, § 709.

[6] Rudolf Ritsema and Shantena Augusto Sabbadini, *The Original I Ching Oracle: The Pure and Complete Texts with Concordance*, Eranos Foundation (SASEF) (London: Watkins Publishing, 2005), p. 9.

[7] *Shu Jing*, ~6th century BCE, text adapted from B. Karlgren, *The Book of Documents*, cited in ibid., p. 2.

[8] Ritsema and Sabbadini, *The Original I Ching Oracle*, p. 2.

[9] *Ibid.*, p. 3.

[10] Jung, "The Stages of Life"[1930-1931], CW 8, § 753.

[11] John-Raphael Staude, *The Adult Development of C.G. Jung* (Boston: Routledge & Kegan Paul, 1981), pp. ix-x.

[12] Jung, "The Stages of Life," CW 8, § 778.

[13] *Ibid.*

[14] *Ibid.*, CW 8, § 772.

[15] *Ibid.*, CW 8, § 773.

[16] *Ibid.*, CW 8, § 773.

[17] *Ibid.*, CW 8, § 787.

[18] Dante Alighieri, "Inferno," Canto 1, *The Divine Comedy* [1308-1321], " trans. Henry Wadsworth Longfellow (Project Gutenberg Digital Edition, 1997), p. 4.

[19] Jung, "The years, of which I have spoken to you..." [1957], in *The Red Book, Liber Novus*, ed. Sonu Samdashni, pref. Ulrich Hoerni, trans. Mark Kyburz, John Peck, Sonu Samdashani, Philemon Series (New York: W.W. Norton & Company), Front Matter, unnumbered page.

[20] Sigmund Freud, "Civilisation and Its Discontents," in *The Standard Edition of the Complete Psychological Works of Sigmund Freud,*

Volume XXI, The Future of An Illusion, Civilisation and Its Discontents and Other Works, 1927-1931, trans. from the German under the general editorship of James Strachey; in collaboration with Anna Freud; assisted by Alix Strachey and Alan Tyson (London: The Hogarth Press and the Institute of Psycho-analysis, 1961), p. 144.

[21] Jung, "Approaching the Unconscious," in *Man and His Symbols* (Garden City, N.Y., Doubleday, 1964), p. 85.

[22] Edward Gibbon, *The History of the Decline and Fall of the Roman Empire*, ed. and abridged by David P. Womersley (New York, NY: Penguin, 2001), p. 435.

[23] William Ophuls, *Immoderate Greatness: Why Civilizations Fail* (North Charleston, SC: CreateSpace Independent Publishing Platform, 2012), back cover.

[24] Fritjof Capra, *The Turning Point* (London: Fontana, 1983), p. 25.

[25] Matt Daily, "Exxon CEO calls climate change engineering problem," June 27, 2012, in *Reuters*, US Edition, at www.reuters.com/article/2012/06/27/us-exxon-climate-idUSBRE85Q1C820120627 (accessed July 22, 2013).

[26] Jung, "The Houston Films" [1957], in *C.G. Jung Speaking: Interviews and Encounters*, eds. William McGuire and R.F.C. Hull (Princeton, N.J. : Princeton University Press, 1977), p. 303.

[27] Kenneth Boulding, cited in David Attenborough, "Planet and Population," speech to the RSA, 11 March 2011, p. 3, at www.populationmatters.org/documents/rsa_speech.pdf (accessed October 3, 2014).

[28] Wouter J. Hanegraaff, *Esotericism and the Academy: Rejected Knowledge in Western Culture* (Cambridge: Cambridge University Press, 2012), p. 295.

[29] Francis Fukuyama, "The End of History?" in *The National Interest*, Summer 1989.

[30] Alfred Korzybski, *Science and Sanity: An Introduction to Non-Aristotelian Systems and General Semantics*, distributed by Institute of General Semantics, 5th Ed. (Brooklyn, NY: International Non-Aristotelian Library Pub. Co., 1931/2000), p. 750.

[31] Jung, "The Sign of the Fishes" [1951], CW 9ii, § 142.

[32] *Ibid.*, "The Psychology of the Transference" [1946], CW 16, § 524.

[33] *Ibid.*, "The Undiscovered Self (Present and Future)" [1957], CW 10, § 585.

[34] E.F. Schumacher, cited by Fritjof Capra in George Sessions (ed.), *Deep Ecology for the 21st Century* (Boston & London: Shambhala, 1995), p. 25.

[35] Edward Whymper, *Scrambles Amongst the Alps, In the Years 1860-69* (Philadelphia: J.P. Lippincott, 1871).

4

Failure
is the End

Bernard Sartorius

I t was rather strange for me to be sitting beside a wood fire in a cozy pub in Cornwall, while outdoors a storm was sweeping through, beautiful and strong, fast-moving, with sunny spells suddenly casting everything, every wave and every cloud, in absolute flashes of light. It was strange to be in such a place, trying to write something intelligent about failure, particularly about its sting: Failure is the end, or, an experience of real failure is followed by nothing. In the surroundings of Cornwall—where the roaming ponies were presenting the storm with their hindquarters—the very notion of failure seemed to be somehow off. The spirit of this place seemed to say, "Failure—so what?" We might ask, from the standpoint of nature, is a storm a failure? Or does hail amount to failure, or a drought? Does failure occur when one animal is killed by another? Does a flower fail when it is eaten by a passing cow? On larger scale, was it failure when, probably because of a huge meteorite, hundreds of species of dinosaurs and other animals disappeared forever—met their definite end? Would it likewise be a failure if the human species would disappear by a natural or man-made cataclysm? The discrepancy I felt between the academic subject of failure and my very natural surroundings could point to an archetypal phenomenon, namely that the very notion of failure is specifically human.

Dreams frequently present scenarios of failure. One misses a train, a plane; one fails examinations; one fails to meet a person, or to relate to her, or to escape from her; one fails to reach a mountaintop, to catch an animal, to be received by Jung, to make love, to have a child—and so many other variations on the motif (all excerpted from real dreams). Such dreams might signal to the dreamers that some kind of conscious integration lies ahead. They could also indicate that failure without a "rescue button" is an *archetypal* psychic reality, an objective potential, rooted in the unconscious. So, besides suggesting the dreamers' unlived potentials, these dreams might also want to say: you have to face the possibility of inevitable, utter failure—you might not succeed. The frequent occurrence of such dreams today might compensate a contemporary ego-consciousness that is particularly keen to achieve success in all domains, or psychologically, to achieve wholeness as only the valuable legitimation of human existence.

Indeed, as far back as one goes in history, for us humans the fear of absolute failure has been an existential experience of paramount importance, and failure thus appears as a frequent motif in myth, religions, and literature. There is, of course, the terrible fate of Sisyphus, who eternally fails to roll a stone up to a hilltop. Then there are the Greek tragedies that depict their heroes in ultimate failure (that's why these dramas are "tragedies"). Grieved at the death of her brother Orestes, Sophocles's Electra is advised, "… when a god sends harm [*blaptei*], not even the strong man can escape."[1] In Christianity, the image of hell and eternal damnation captures this possibility of basically failed life. The conception of basic, eternal failure was already evident in the Egyptian *Book of the Dead* of the New Kingdom period. With some analogy to the Christian Last Judgment, it describes a netherworld monster who devours those souls whose hearts, weighed on the scale of judgment, fail to measure an adequate quantity of *maat* or justice. As the Qu'ran similarly holds,

> The reward [for lost souls] is that upon them is the curse of
> Allah, the angels and all mankind. They shall remain under
> it for ever; neither will their punishment be lightened nor
> will they be given respite.[2]

And if we jump over the centuries to a quasi contemporary work
cherished by us Jungians, we find the Grimm's fairy tales to be packed
with characters embodying absolute failure. Rumpelstiltskin tears
himself to shreds when his name is discovered and thus his scheme to
obtain the princess's child comes to naught.[3] In "The Devil with the
Three Golden Hairs," the greedy King who tries, unsuccessfully, to
prevent his daughter's marriage is cursed to forever ferry people across
the river to hell.[4] Innumerable wicked stepmothers and witches fall
into similar fates, all ending badly—burned alive, hanged, and so on.
Like the souls lost forever in hell, they too stand for the potential of
absolute failure.

Coming from a variety of cultural contexts and periods, these
few examples commonly hold some key elements that could point
to the archetypal quality of failure. Most essentially, the motif
pertains less to the failure to accomplish a specific task or goal, than
to the failure of *life as such*. The end in hell or in the bowels of an
underworld monster amounts to a life lost in relationship to the
gods, to God, to *maat*, to individuation, or to some other ego-
transcending force. Jesus seems to allude to the potential when he
asks, "For what is a man profited, if he shall gain the whole world,
and lose his own soul?"[5]

By the very horror of their outcomes, the symbolic scenarios evoke
the idea that failure is psychologically unacceptable. Yet as they
dramatize the ultimate ends, the stories also *compensate* the fantasy
that life should be successful—that we should succeed in all areas,
including, for instance, extraverted social relationships and the more
introverted relationship with "god" or with the Self as the utmost source
of meaning. The powerful ego fantasy of success makes the fantasy of
ultimate failure inevitable. And the severity of the failure fantasy
increases in proportion to the grandiosity of the success fantasy, a
phenomenon that expresses itself among other ways in the relative
closeness of hell and paradise: The ancient Greeks located in relative
proximity to each other the sinful souls in the underground Tartarus
and the virtuous souls not in the sky, but in the Elysian Fields, "in

the far west of the inhabited earth." By contrast, Christians envision an infinite distance between hell far below and heaven way above.

The dramatization of success and failure need not appear in familiar mythic images like heaven and hell. In the present time, success takes the rational guise of efficiency ensured by technology and technological mindsets. The mythical quality appears in the quasi totalitarian way in which efficiency is preached, enforced, and held as an ultimate measure of success. But there is a major difference between the traditional and contemporary imagery: Being non- and even anti-religious, today's western civilization and its imitators are compelled to suppress and ban to the unconscious "hell" and other notions and images of absolute failure. Consequently this civilization is equally pressed to attribute an almost absolute mythical importance to failure—be it relational, technical, scholarly, administrative, or otherwise.

If one indeed experiences absolute failure in an important realm of life, one might at least sense the archetypal psychic abyss, the objective possibility of unavoidable failure. To amplify this idea, let us refer to the well-known New Testament parable about the sower:

> Behold, there went out a sower to sow: And it came to pass, as he sowed, some [seed] fell by the way side, and the fowls of the air came and devoured it up. And some fell on stony ground, where it had not much earth; and immediately it sprang up, because it had no depth of earth: But when the sun was up, it was scorched; and because it had no root, it withered away. And some fell among thorns, and the thorns grew up, and choked it, and it yielded no fruit. And others fell on good ground, and did yield fruit that sprang up and increased; and brought forth, some thirty, and some sixty, and some an hundred. And [Jesus] said unto them, He that hath ears to hear, let him hear.[6]

The parable illuminates the objective, inescapable failure, that is, the failure that occurs utterly independently of human will or liability. Yet the story is often interpreted moralistically, teaching that we are supposed to make efforts to become the good soil rather than the rocky or the thorny ground. But the point Jesus wanted to make is a different one: For reasons that are *unknowable and unavoidable*, it happens that the seeds fall either on good soil or on bad soil. For reasons that are unknowable and unavoidable, so many seeds fail while others succeed,

even multiplying "by some thirty, and some sixty, and an hundred."
In other words, the parable sheds light on a level of reality in which it
is beside the point to look for etiological explanations as to why there
is failure or success. The objective potential for absolute failure is thus
dramatically underlined and seems to make irrelevant all consideration
of conscious culpability. In his own commentary, Jesus hints at some
reasons for this, yet without implying the demand for a willful change
in our ego attitude or morals. The seeds devoured by the birds might
illustrate that insights "sown in our hearts" may be swallowed up, for
instance by unconscious impulses; the seeds falling on rocky soil
describe the situation in which people "receive" the truth "with
gladness" but "have no roots in themselves," and so falter when this
truth is challenged; the seeds falling into the thorns allude to truth
that is heard but overshadowed by material "lusts" and worries about
day-to-day survival; and finally, concerning those who receive and keep
the truth, Jesus simply remarked that they are "the good soil."[7]

The parable leaves us insecure, rightly so, about our ability to
consciously influence the success or failure of our lives or our
individuation. Is it just so, that I am "bad soil"? Can I *do* anything to
have a really successful life, or—from the viewpoint of the Self—a
meaningful one? Even if I could grasp the meaning of my dreams, do
they always help? On first glance, some of the evoked mythologies seem
to imply that we can indeed take responsibility for our own fate. For
instance, in ancient Egypt, the soul continued its voyage to paradise
if the weighing of heart revealed an earthly life lived with adequate
justice (*maat*). In Islam it is often said that sinners bring upon
themselves Allah's scorn and retribution. Many Christians maintain
that the way to heaven is paved by one's earthly good works, genuine
repentance, and unquestioning belief in the triune God. But on
the other hand, in ancient Greece it was *moira*—fate itself—that
pushed souls toward tragic and ultimate failure, whether they felt
blameworthy or not. In the Old Testament, it is Yaweh who
"hardens the [Pharaoh's] heart," so that the Pharaoh "shall not let
the [Hebrews] go" until he suffers the death of his own "first-born
[son]."[8] The Qu'ran often asserts that the *kufr*, the unbelievers, are
infidels not by their own doing, but because "Allah wants to lead them
astray."[9] The sixteenth-century Church Reformer John Calvin preached
a doctrine that continues to imagine *predestined* salvation for some

people and eternal damnation for others. Thus, we have an array of paradoxical and contradictory pathways that open an empty space in the fantasy of our supposed self-determination.

There is in this connection Freud's reflection that seems to dissolve the very question of subjective consciousness and responsibility in these matters. In 1915, during World War I, he wrote,

> That which we call our "unconscious," the deepest layers of our souls, consisting of drives, is aware of absolutely nothing negative, no negation—the opposites collapse in [the unconscious]—and it is therefore unaware of … death, which we can only see as a negative content…. Perhaps this is even the secret of heroism.[10]

In other words, the archetypal images of hell and our imagined responsibility for avoiding it or not could belong to some extent to our unconscious projections and hopes for a successful life. Yet such expectations might be rather superficial, rather close to the ego, when viewed in relationship to a much deeper unknown, to the deeply unconscious, which itself would mirror pure nature (like a storm, the disappearance of the dinosaurs, death and its aftermath, and the like). Later we will come back to the idea that our conscious influence on life fulfillment will never be in our own hands.

Before going on, let's try to see how we might typically behave when confronted with the risk of failed life or individuation, a landing in hell. Deprived of confidence in self-determination, we are at the very least filled with dreadful uncertainty. Such ego reactions can be discerned in the previously mentioned story of Sisyphus, now summarized here:

> King Sisyphus and his brother Salmoneus were the sons of King Aeolus of Thessaly and Corinth. During his reign, Sisyphus promoted navigation and trade. He was said to be not only versatile but also deceitful to the point of violating Zeus's domain and the laws of hospitality by killing travellers and guests in order to maintain his power. In a plot against his hated his brother Salmoneus, Sisyphus seduced his niece, Salmoneus's daughter Tyro. Tyro slayed the children she bore by Sisyphus when she discovered his scheme to use them to assassinate Salmoneus. Not only did Sisyphus commit incest and plot to murder his brother. He again betrayed Zeus by disclosing to the river god Asopus the place where Zeus had hidden Asopus's daughter after

abducting her. In return, Asopus saw to it that a spring would begin to flow from the Corinthian Acropolis. With this, Zeus had had enough. So he ordered Thanatos—death—to chain up Sisyphus. But, cleverly, Sisyphus asked Thanatos to demonstrate the handling of the chains and used the knowledge to trap Thanatos instead. Sisyphus's trick provoked an uproar among the gods because, without Thanatos, humans would no longer die and the world would soon be overrun. The god of war Ares, particularly displeased, freed Thanatos and handed Sisyphus over to him. But once more, now in the underworld, Sisyphus persuaded Persephone, the queen of Tartarus, to set him free again. Now enough was enough. As punishment for all his offenses, Sisyphus was condemned by the gods to eternally roll a huge stone up a steep hill, only to watch it roll down again, over and over, until the end of time.[11]

We might be prone to say that, given Sisyphus's offenses to men and the gods, he deserves his eternal punishment. However, abstaining from moral judgment, we find that Sisyphus could well symbolize an ordinary, non-idealized ego. The myth depicts him negatively, narrating his sins, because the reality of a true, genuine, fully historical life stands in conflict with another archetypal aspect of the psyche: The tendency to idealize, a tendency that sustains our permanent fantasy of how things, ourselves, and others should be—in any case different from how they are now. Sisyphus is a king, symbolically an image of the "ruling" function of ego consciousness. Typical ego features are suggested in Sisyphus's urge to power and control, and in his material gains (from trade and navigation). The ego is full of desires and wants them satisfied—even to the point of expecting bounty from the unconscious, such as that symbolized in the spring brought to flow on the Acropolis's high ground. Sisyphus's greed might allude to the naturally conservative quality of ego consciousness and its definition of "the normal" as "the good," which must be preserved. Let us consider, too, Sisyphus's rivalry with his brother Salmoneus. The Greek root *sal* indicates agitation, and could allude to the shadowy restlessness of the ego striving to keep things under control, an ego rivaling to be "on top." Shaped in childhood, this kind of ego drive necessarily contains an incestuous component, which appears symbolically in Sisyphus's seduction of Tyro, his own niece, his brother's daughter. Another ego trait comes to light in Sisyphus's scheme to consolidate his power by instrumentalizing the children he begot with Tyro. This all points to a natural, regressive, childish component typically at work in ego assertions. Last but not least, another ego property is symbolized as profit gained from the disclosure of the gods' secrets, here, the secret related to one of Zeus' love affairs. Such profiteering reflects the human drive for self-gain—if need be, at the expense of loyalty to God, the gods, and/or nature. Likewise, Prometheus steals the fire from Zeus; Adam and Eve consume the forbidden apple; and Sisyphus procures a spring on a mountaintop (the latter which perhaps speaks for our own trade and the psychologist's use of rational theories and methods to dredge up the elusive life of the psyche).

Sisyphus's profile suggests that, by its very nature, ego consciousness is compelled to overstep god-given boundaries. Such boundaries might first be felt in limits that frustrate or thwart the satisfaction of every-day desires and that can thus give rise to experiences of mild failure. Managing to achieve his own escape from Thanatos and Tartarus, Sisyphus personifies the ego's inability to accept death—death itself being the utmost and final failure of the drive to life. So, on the whole, Sisyphus appears as an icon of the ego's normal way of coping: striving for success, exploiting all means to satisfy needs and desires, attempting to avert mild failure and to escape final defeat. This permanent need to be in control is a major ego quality—and I do mean *quality*, because it is an intrinsic part of being human. Sisyphus's endless rolling of the stone suggests that our desire to control and succeed, one hundred percent, condemns us to permanent fantasies of failure. So the recurring experience of failure—the small, the large, and the ultimate—is inscribed in the very nature of ego psychology.

Yet we find a spark of hope in a remarkable feature of Sisyphus's endlessly failing efforts to keep his stone on the hilltop, a hope that lies in the very *repetitiveness* of his task. Repetition as such is an archetypal motif, which develops the basic structures of dance, music, architecture, religious ritual; it appears as well in fairy tales, myths, and biblical stories. Repetition can participate in a psychic constellation whereby ego consciousness is brought to the end of its possibilities and induced to move beyond the dichotomy of failure and success. Entering into this beyond, I might encounter happily unexpected change—a new life, a true partner, life after death—but not *necessarily*. Let us not be mistaken: Although it *might* contribute to an opening of consciousness, repetition cannot be used purposely like a tool with the conscious intent to reach this opening. It is usually only when we have not asked for it that repetition exhausts our ego achievements and desires for the sake of fostering a widening of consciousness.

As a Sisyphus-like repetition of failure might induce a change of consciousness that transcends the sharp dichotomy of failure and success, it could as well engender consciousness of "hell," awareness of utter failure and its latent recurrence. In other words, viewed from the basic framework of individuation, failure and success are *not necessarily* complementary. It is not in the nature of failure to lead to success. Can we really envisage Jesus's failure and resurrection in the same way that we see pairs of complementary opposites in day and night, light and darkness, yin and yang, good and evil, creation and destruction, masculine and feminine, conscious and unconscious? We could indeed imagine a nice dialectical connection between failure and success, each pole needing the other. However in the end, the archetype would be "bleached," maybe not as brightly as the slogan would hastily have it, "Failure is the door to success." But the horror of hell would be unrealistically mellowed. Jung seems to hint at this issue when he discerns the "shocking paradox" in visions like those of Jakob Böhme's, which "propound ... God's love glowing in the midst of hellfire."[12] The paradox is "shocking" because we are not inclined to apprehend hellfire and love together, in close proximity, or in the one God. The image as such defies our sense of God's presence in paradise and radical absence in hell, the psychic state we can envision to be completely devoid of connection with the Self. It could well be that we reach a level of reality that renders meaningless any talk about a complementary, dialectical pair of opposites. There could be an *infinite* gap between success (as symbolized in paradise, eternal life, resurrection, and the like)—and absolute failure (as symbolized in images of hell, and as expressed in Jesus's desperate cry on the cross, "my God, my God, why did you fail me?"). It would be a yawning chasm that makes it impossible to imagine, at this level of reality, a pair of complementary opposites.

There are indeed archetypal images of such a break between absolute failure and success. Among the sources is the ancient Egyptian "Amduat" (less commonly knowns as the "Imydwat"), one of the *Books of the Dead* from the New Kingdom Period. As the text describes the soul's twelve-hour sojourn in the Underworld, the "fifth hour" could be highly significant for our consideration of a *most fundamental* gap between failure and success.[13] For the fifth hour—transpiring nearly mid-way through the journey—evokes radical uncertainty as to whether the soul will continue its voyage toward new life or remain forever in hell, utterly failed.

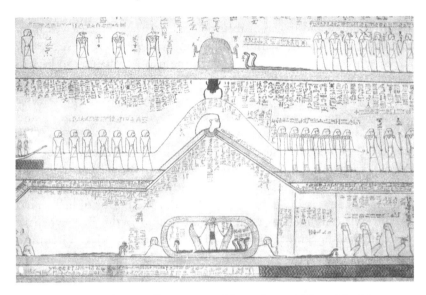

Figure 1. *Imydwat, Fifth Hour*, Detail from KV 35, Valley of the Kings East Valley, Thebes (Photograph by Francis Dzikowski, April 1999, Image 14673, © Theban Mapping Project)

The above image shows the fifth hour to contain a sun barque or boat, which is carrying the deceased's soul and being pulled over "waters that are fire."[14] Sokar, the god ruling over this hour, is said to be "unknown," "invisible," "imperceptible,"[15] and "secret"[16]—all attributes of his wholly ineffable nature. At the same time he is an ancient earth god connected with fertility and death. As the text says, the soul is now "on the secret path of the Land of Sokar."[17] Isis (the feminine profile in the center of the picture) is the goddess under whose patronage the fifth hour unfolds, and for this reason the image of her head crowns the whole scenario. Here Isis possibly embodies the feminine and unavoidable acceptance of absolute failure as a real possibility. As this fundamental question mark is symbolically located in a secret space, one can venture to say that any conscious interpretation of what happens here would be mistaken.

The drawing in the *Amduat* depicts the secret space itself in the oval-shaped cartouche inhabited by a snake with heads at opposite ends. Thus three snake heads looking toward the right and a human head looking toward the left enable this creature to move backward and forward—to return to "ground zero," so to speak, or to move onward and ahead. Called "the greatest god, he who extends his wings," this snake, according to some Egyptologists, possibly alludes to original chaos when everything and nothing was possible.[18] The secret god Sokar stands above this totally mysterious god of chaos, holding his wings, as if to lead him. And here we should note: original chaos does not necessarily produce anything new...

So, in the main features of this "fifth hour" we have sufficient evidence for the *possibility* of a gulf between a permanent hell and a moving-beyond-it. That is, the totally unknowable snake god facing opposite directions—and the wholly secret Sokar symbolizing life and death—could reveal the deep psychic fact of a "black hole" of absolute uncertainty between ultimate failure (death, hell, no individuation) and success (life, paradise, individuation). Here Jung's *deo concedente*—by God's grace—gains its full weight. The opposites, success and failure, do not *necessarily* produce a *conjunctio* or a transcendent "third." Failure *might* be definitive. The hieroglyphic text resonates with the aura of this complete mystery:

> The image is like this in the Unified Darkness. The oval belonging to this god [Sokar] is illuminated by the two eyes of the great god (the serpent). [Sokar's] two feet shine in the coils of the great god, while [Sokar] protects his image. A noise is heard…, after this great god has passed…, like the thundering sound of the sky during a storm.[19]

As the snake's eyes cast the only light in this space, we can imagine that this god alone knows which souls will escape the abyss and which will remain in it forever.

Commenting on an alchemical text, Jung was aware of the potential for a definite gulf between failure and success in the individuation process:

> The centering of the image on hell, which at the same time is
> God, is grounded on the experience that highest and lowest
> both come from the depths of the soul, and either bring the
> frail vessel of consciousness to shipwreck or carry it safely to port,
> with little or no assistance from us. The experience of this "centre"
> [*sic*] is therefore numinous in its own right.[20]

One could not better describe the *numinosum* that infuses the Amduat's
fifth hour, this, too, symbolizing an underworld center that is
absolutely outside of and beyond an ontological complementarity
between basic failure and basic success. The intense numinosity stems
perhaps in part from our human befallenness to the gods' freedom to
decide, and from the inescapable not-knowing that occupies the gap
between our continuing evolution and absolute failure.

Writing on renewal in psychic life, Jung quoted from an alchemical
text, "'But Jesus ... smashed open the iron gates of hell, that the souls
might be saved...'"[21] This passage proposes, again, a resolution of
the polarities of failure and success by the grace of God. In the
Qu'ran, we find a similar motif, where the gap and also human
culpability are emphasized in a particularly strong way. Here, "the
unlucky ones" have no possibility to escape damnation except that
God alone decides otherwise:

> Those who are damned shall be in the fire; in there, they shall
> have only sighs and sobs. They will dwell therein as long as the
> heavens and earth shall last unless [Allah] ordains otherwise;
> surely [your Lord] is the mighty doer of what he intends.[22]

Neither success nor a continuing life with God is guaranteed, for, as
Allah says, "We created man from a sperm containing [everything],
so that we may test him."[23]

* * *

Given the archetypal possibility of absolute failure and the
apparent limits on our own culpability for it, it can well be asked,
with what conscious attitude might we best meet the dead ends? We
might ordinarily idealize, moralize, or maybe adopt a mode of
positive thinking. But we could perhaps more sensibly respond with
humor. As the painter Paul Klee noted in his diary, it can help "'[t]o

laugh, as if death were tickling us with his scythe.'"[24] Think, too, of fairy tales like the Grimm's "Brother Lustig." Literally translated, "Brother Jolly" or "Brother Funny," is the trickster who arrives in heaven by outwitting St. Peter along the whole way.[25] In another tale laughter comes to the rescue when a band of elves abducts a child, leaving a changeling in the cradle:

> The changeling, who had "a large head and staring eyes," just lay there, "and would do nothing but eat and drink." The fretting mother follows her neighbor's seemingly absurd advice that "all would be over with him" if she could make him laugh by boiling water in two empty egg shells. And laugh he did, when all of a sudden the elves appeared, returned the real child, and absconded with the changeling.[26]

Humor abounds in the tale that features the comical naivety of the spirit who, upon his release from entrapment in a bottle, grows to a tremendous size and announces himself to be the "mighty Mercurius." As Mercurius is about to strangle his liberator, the poor boy deters him by saying,

> "Slowly … not so fast. I must first know that you were really shut up in that little bottle, and that you are the right spirit. If indeed, you can get in again, I will believe, and then you my do as you will with me." The spirit said haughtily, "that is a very trifling feat," drew himself together, and made himself as small and slender as he had been at first, so that he crept … right through the neck of the bottle in again. Scarcely was he within than the boy thrust the cork … back into the bottle, … and the spirit was deceived.[27]

These are but several tales that propose humor as an adequate response to archetypal failure or its imminence, and to the hermeneutical chasm we experience with this reality. In his acceptance speech for the National Book Award in 1955 William Faulkner uttered with "droll humor,"

> "Even failure is worthwhile and admirable, provided only that the failure is splendid enough, the dream splendid enough, unattainable enough, yet forever valuable enough, since it was of perfection… ."[28]

* * *

Moving toward a conclusion, let us recap and further reflect:

The very likely reality of an archetype of failure compels us to take seriously the potential of failing absolutely. With this, life gains a certain weight and *tremendum*, a tendency to invoke fear and trembling, which most of the time is pushed into the unconscious. As we have noted, however, that which appears as ultimate failure can be seen as a gateway to success. But our belief in this *a priori* perception would in fact water down our adequate fear of absolute failure—and it would be precisely our non-belief in absolute failure that makes such failure all the more possible. So, essential failure confronts us with a paradox that resonates like a koan: If I do not acknowledge that the door might be definitely locked, it will definitely not open. There is no recipe that helps us to deal with this dilemma. It posits a mercurial, perhaps dangerous riddle and a fundamental ethical question, which we each must resolve in our individual ways.

Concrete failure—be it relational, professional, or practical (such as losing a parking place)—may touch our narcissistic sense of need or wounding. But it might also conjure up the possibility of ultimate failure in one's life and individuation and, beyond this, death as the failed drive to live. Of course one's awareness of such grievous failure becomes clearer in the second half of life, after youth and young adulthood have necessarily focused on immediate failures and successes.

Religious traditions that symbolize experiences of hell illustrate in particularly clear ways the reality of absolute failure. Moreover they insist that the conscious ego refrain from evaluation. "Judge not, and ye shall not be judged," Jesus said.[29] His words are echoed in innumerable passages of the Qu'ran, which assert that it is God who knows best what constitutes ultimate failure and success, and who is condemned to hell, blessed with paradise, or obtains the possibility to move in between.[30] (For us analysts, the suspension of subjective judgment virtually excludes our evaluation of our clients' success or failure to individuate—which is not to mention the questionability of our own self-evaluations.)

As concerns our attitude toward death, if we honestly attempt to lay aside avoidance strategies, we cannot help but see it as the ultimate failure of the natural desire to live. At this point we must again recall the "gap" between "hell" and "paradise." If there is any "beyond" to death, seen rightly so as the definitive failure of the will to life, this "beyond" cannot belong to a mythological or imaginary realm of any kind. In very early narratives of what happened after the Crucifixion—before the account was "mythologized"—the risen Christ appears as a simple fellow traveller or a gardener.[31] That is to say, he manifested in a radically *non-mythological* shape, and, precisely because of it, those who encountered him did not recognize him.

Acknowledgment of the archetypal possibility of absolute failure underlines the difference in spirit between analysis and psychotherapy. To put it bluntly, psychotherapy *needs* success, envisioned as the reduction or disappearance of patients' symptoms, their discovery of new meanings, their achievement of better socialization, better partnerships, and so on. In this sense, psychotherapy is more suitable for the first half of life. On the other hand, analysis does not exclude but also does not require success, because it opens the analysand to acceptance of the archetypal potential for failure. This opening is more frequently and consciously experienced in the second half of life, even more towards life's end, when the totally unknown lingers on the horizon. Whether or not we analysts can truly open to this dimension is in question. The difficulty of doing so might partly explain why many of us at times prefer or indefinitely maintain a psychotherapeutic perspective.

The issue of our conscious responsibility for failure remains an open one. Our smile or even laughter about this seemingly impossible situation might be the adequate reaction and perhaps even a sign that we have sacrificed the youthful pretense to be always on top, always a winner. We begin, perhaps, to agree with the cartoonist Sipress, who in one drawing portrays two seasoned tramps resting against an abandoned old building. The one, his finger raised in an "aha" moment, says to the other, "… Hey, hold on a minute—maybe failure is an option."[32]

* * *

Allow me to conclude with an extremely short fairy-tale. In a single paragraph it relays the story of a poor boy who stumbles upon a tiny golden key. Soon he finds the iron chest to which it belongs. As he is carefully sliding the tiny key into the nearly invisible keyhole, the tale ends, "and now we have to wait…"[33] Thus waited the ocean waves, the ponies, the intermittent sunrays, and inside the pub, the flames of the fireplace—and maybe the Celtic souls at the bar—as I was pondering the subject of failure...

Al hamdul'Illah

NOTES

¹ Sophocles, "Electra," in *The Greek Classics, Sophocles—Seven Plays*, trans. The Athenian Society, ed. James H. Ford, First Ed. (El Paso, TX: El Paso Norte Press, 2006), p. 145. In the cited passage, "harm" is the translation of the original Greek, *blaptei*, that is, to harm someone by making him fail.

² *Qu'ran*, Surah 3:87-88, trans. Malik, at Alim.org, http://www.alim.org/library/quran/ayah/compare/3/87/curse-of-allah,-the-angels-and-all-mankind-on-the-unbelievers-and-fate-of-the-unbelievers-who-die-as-unbelievers (accessed October 23, 2014). All future references to the Surah are from this source.

³ Grimm, *The Complete Grimm's Fairy Tales*, "Rumplestiltskin," Nr. 55 (London: Routledge and Kegan Paul, 1975).

⁴ Ibid., "The Devil with the Three Golden Hairs," Nr. 29.

⁵ *The Holy Bible*, King James Version, Matthew 16:26. All future references to the Bible are from this source.

⁶ Ibid., Mark 4:3-9.

⁷ Ibid., 4:13-20.

⁸ Ibid., Exodus 4:21-22.

⁹ Surah 11:34; see also 14:4.

¹⁰ Sigmund Freud, "Unser Verhältniss zum Tod," originally published in *Imago* Vol. IV, 1915, reproduced in *Gesammelte Werke* Band 10 (Frankfurt s/M: Fischer-Verlag, 1991), p. 350. My translation from the original German:

> Was wir unser "Unbewusstes" heissen, die tiefsten, aus Triebregungen bestehenden Schichten unserer Seele, kennt überhaupt nichts Negatives, keine Verneinung—Gegensätze fallen in ihm zusammen—und kennt darum auch nicht den eigenen Tod, dem wir nur einen negativen Inhalt geben können. ... Vielleicht ist dies sogar das Geheimniss des Heldentums.

[11] "Sisyphus," in *Wikipedia, The Free Encyclopedia*, at http://en.wikipedia.org/wiki/Sisyphus (accessed October 25, 2014), my paraphrase.

[12] C.G. Jung, "The Ambivalence of the Fish Symbol," in *Aion* [1951/1959], *The Collected Works of C.G. Jung*, Vol. 9ii, eds. Sir Herbert Read, Michael Fordham, Gerhard Adler, William McGuire, trans. R.F.C. Hull, Bollingen Series XX, 2nd Ed., 5th Printing (Princeton: Princeton University Press, 1978), § 191. Future references to Jung's *Collected Works* will be abbreviated, with chapter titles followed by the volume and paragraph numbers.

[13] Erik Hornung, *The Ancient Egyptian Books of the Afterlife*, trans. David Lorton (New York: Cornell University Press, 1999), see pp. 27-53.

[14] Erik Hornung, "Amduat," in *Ägyptische Unterweltsbücher*, trans. Erik Hornung (Damstadt: Wissenschaftliche Buchgesellschaft, 1984), p. 115; my translation here and in other references to this source.

[15] *Ibid.*, p. 104.

[16] *Ibid.*, p. 110.

[17] *Ibid.*, p. 112.

[18] See for instance, Siegfried Schott, *Zum Weltbild der Jenseits—Führer des Neuen Reichs*, quoted in *ibid.*, p. 113.

[19] David Warburton, *The Egyptian Amduat, The Book of the Hidden Chamber*, trans. David Warburton, eds. Erik Hornung, Theodor Abt, Rev. Ed. (Einsiedeln: Daimon Verlag, 2007), p. 171, at *The Egyptian Amduat, The Book of the Hidden Chamber Book Gallery*, ©2014 Amduat.com & Rostau.com, John D. Jefferson, clostchord.com/amduat5html (accessed October 25, 2014).

[20] Jung, "The Ambivalence," CW 9ii, § 209.

[21] Text quoted in Jung, *"Mysterium Conjunctionis III,"* *Gesammelte Werke*, Band 14 (Olten and Freiburg i.B.: Walter-Verlag, 1984), p. 365; my translation of the German.

[22] Surah 11:106-107.

[23] *Ibid.*, 76:2.

[24] Heinrich Heine, quoted in Paul Klee, *The Diaries of Paul Klee, 1898–1918*, ed. Felix Klee, trans. authorized by Felix Klee (Berkeley: University of California Press, 1968), § 607.

[25] Grimm, "Brother Lustig," No. 81.

[26] *Ibid.*, "The Elves, Third Story," No. 39, p. 200, with my paraphrase.

[27] *Ibid.*, "The Spirit in the Bottle," No. 99, p. 460.

[28] William Faulkner, quoted in Mary Stahlman Douglas, "Editor Twice Met Faulkner at National Books Awards," in *Conversations with William Faulkner*, ed. M. Thomas Inge (Jackson: University of Mississippi Press, 1999), pp. 113-114.

[29] *The Holy Bible*, Luke 6:37.

[30] See for instance Surah, 2:24, 6:13, and 40:20.

[31] *The Holy Bible*, respectively, Luke 24:13-18 and John 20:15.

[32] Sipress, TCB-123651.jpg, in *The New Yorker Cartoon Bank*, *The Condé Nast Collection*, at www.cartoonbank.com/home (accessed November 6, 2014).

[33] Grimm, "The Golden Key," Nr. 200, p. 812.

5

The Implications of Shame
for the Analytical Process

Ursula Lenz Bücker

My contribution to the Jungian Odyssey in Grindelwald and now to this volume derives from my effort to understand archetypal patterns that constitute stalemates in analysis. I have come to the conclusion that many situations of prolonged speechlessness and lack of self-awareness are due to a profound disregard of the issue of shame.

My professional exposure to shame started with my practice in a clinic for forensic psychiatry. I worked in a high security area where there was a prevalent potential for violent acting out due to unbearable inner tension or unbearable shame. Here I experienced the dilemma of protecting both my colleagues' safety and my patients' inner development, of meeting legal objectives, and of taking care of myself in a very down-to-earth way. Although the staff was given some framework for the conduct of dangerous situations, much was left to the professionally accountable therapist on duty. Thus arose my general professional interest in shame and its phenomenology, its psychology. But my interest now reaches far beyond (arbitrary) definitions of shame's subtle expressions and destructive and seductive powers. Today I essentially search for ways to deal with the truth that shame is failure's venom. A quote that is popularly attributed to Jung contains the core of the matter: "Shame is a soul eating emotion."

The etymology of the word "shame" covers a vast variety of languages with Proto-Indo-European background as well as Persian and Albanian roots. The generally shared understanding of shame implies the meanings of "insult, offence, cover, and shroud," and refers to "an uncomfortable, painful and infiltrating feeling due to recognition or consciousness of impropriety, dishonor or other wrong." Related to these meanings, I experienced growing reluctance to expose my patients' case material to a general public. So, when I come to illustrate here, I will use mainly literary examples.

Shame is not a modern phenomenon; it has been described as the glue holding together people, families, and societies. Being ashamed, losing face, is a cross-cultural reality. The Haida, a North American First Nation, put it this way: "To lose one's face is to lose one's spirit, which is truly the 'face,' the dancing mask, the right to incarnate a spirit and wear an emblem or totem."[1] Thus it is not astonishing that we find collective traces in ancient texts like the Bible, too. One of the most famous passages, about 2500 years old, points to a core issue of shame, namely the dilemma and tension caused by its huge induced feeling of invisibility juxtaposed with the profound longing to be seen:

> And they heard the voice of the LORD GOD walking in the cool of the day. And Adam and his wife hid themselves for the presence of our LORD GOD amongst the trees of the garden…. And he said, I heard thy voice in the garden, and I was afraid, because I *was* naked.[2]

The following biblical passage might reflect the long-lasting impact of shame and the even divine effort needed to restore the freely vibrant psyche:

> Fear not; for thou shalt not be ashamed: neither be thou confounded; for thou shalt not be put to shame: for thou shalt forget the shame of thy youth; and shalt not remember the reproach of thy widowhood anymore.[3]

The enfeebling dynamic of shame that we witness in these ancient texts and know from many patients' lives, and that leads from grievances about frail health into the experienced void of depression, can be re-discovered in William Shakespeare's famous words,

> Cowards die many times before their deaths;
> The valiant never taste death but once.[4]

Shame is the herald of standstill or the disruption of the continuity of being.

Another well-known literary example appears in Jane Austen's *Pride and Prejudice,* where the main character Elizabeth Bennet first experiences overwhelming shame in the course of searching for a husband, and afterwards comes to a moment of psychological insight:

> "How despicably I have acted," she cried, "I, who have prided myself on my discernment... . How humiliating is this discovery! Yet, how just a humiliation! Had I been in love, I could not have been more wretchedly blind. But vanity, not love, has been my folly.... Till this moment, I never knew myself."[5]

Many of the complexities of this novel arise from the antinomies of wounded pride and mortifying shame. What we can discern in this short episode are essential archetypal elements of shame, in particular *pride* or *self-esteem* succumbing to the feelings of *insufficiency, disguising, exposure, unveiling,* and *pain.*

Turning to a more modern literary example, I cite from Joseph Conrad's novel *Lord Jim*, written in 1900. There you find the struggle triggered by the mix of shame with its countermovement pride, which in this narrative leads the main character into a desperate dead-end and finally to death:

> Then Jim understood. He had retreated from one world, for a small matter... , and now the other, the work of his own hands, had fallen in ruins upon his head.... Everything was gone.... Loneliness was closing on him. People had trusted him with their lives—only for that; and yet they could never, as he had said, never be made to understand him.... "I have no life," he said... . Whether he had any hope—what he expected, what he imagined—it is impossible to say. He was inflexible, and with the growing loneliness of his obstinacy his spirit seemed to rise above the ruins of his existence.... "There is nothing to fight for.... There is no escape.... Nothing can touch me," he said in a last flicker of superb egoism.... And that's the end. He passes away under a cloud, inscrutable at heart, forgotten, unforgiven, and excessively romantic. Not in the wildest days of his boyish visions could he have seen the alluring shape of such an extraordinary success! ... We can see him, an obscure conqueror of fame, tearing

himself out of the arms of a jealous love at the sign, at the call of
his exalted egoism. He goes away from a living woman to celebrate
his pitiless wedding with a shadowy ideal of conduct.[6]

Shame—hidden shame—is one of the most profound and subtle
reactions to failure and presumed failure in everyday life as well as in
the analytical encounter. It tends to be within arm's length of both
the patient's biographical experience and the analytical encounter itself.
It seems to be at least one of the most pervasive and infiltrating
occurrences in relationships. It invades the body and is stored on a
cellular basis, often beyond verbal access. This is due to the fact that
our implicit knowledge of shame and its very antagonist, pride, forms
in earliest life. Think of a baby's squeal of pleasure, emitted when she
or he achieves new skills and the matching attention and reflection in
the Other's "beaming eye," versus the shame induced by neglect,
ignorance, or rejection.

In the therapeutic realm shame reveals itself to be intertwined with
all kinds of psychic problems and disorders, especially with trauma
and no less with many somatic diseases. Wherever shame happens it
silences the soul and the inner flow of energy. The shamed or shameful
person becomes disconnected from her or his inner resources and
excluded from the empathic touch of the outer world. Shame induces
one's overwhelming self-perceptions of powerlessness, impotence,
helplessness, and ugliness. Shame is linked to failing attunement,
which tends to happen in lacks of resonance or in mismatching
resonance with the Other. It happens in utter silence within a person,
most often not notably on the surface. Shame is the emotion most
commonly found at the very bottom of "psychic collapse," a
parasympathetic response to the threat of (psychic) death. Psyche
comes to total arrest while the body prepares for death. In contrast to
the sufferer's common reactions of subtle disgust and turning away,
the therapist aims at a reversal of this fatal pattern, intending to express
courage and devotion toward the inner struggle for life and to help
the patient discover this kind of attitude.

Shame can be evoked by any real, vicarious, or feared embarrassment,
perplexity, clumsiness, dilemma, constraint, bias, shyness, impasse,
and the like. And it can go to the extent of developing pervasive, *original*
shame. No longer connected to specific triggering events, original
shame resembles a vast void, felt as forlorn, archaic despair. The void

and despair arise largely—if not only—from an on-going, painful interplay between the hiding and uncovering of previous mortifications and humiliations. Jung himself describes the condition as,

> an indefinable but excruciating emptiness. . . . [N]o starting point exists—it would first have to be created. Here a special introversion of the libido is necessary, supported perhaps by favorable external conditions, such as complete rest, especially at night, when the libido has in any case a tendency to introversion.[7]

Jung's advice to write down the inner experience can be translated into the necessity to employ any creative means that can contain and empathetically witness the inner truth. In this way, one facilitates the creation or re-creation of a "larger narrative" of meaningfulness and the emergence of a sacred space or temenos.[8]

Many constellations that lead into analysis can be understood as failing or misguided efforts that veil some other unconscious and unresolved problem. Symptoms, even shaming ones, can hide yet larger shaming issues, e.g. relational trauma, abandonment, unresolved mortal rage, overwhelming guilt, paralyzing anxiety, or—closer to the void—an absence of meaning.

In analytical work shame usually comes in disguise. The Freudian analyst Leon Wurmser, one of the outstanding thinkers on shame, holds that some of its "masks" manifest in patients who seem either very distanced, far away, even beyond reach—or way too close, overwhelming, and distracting with tiniest details.[9] Some patients might unwittingly hide behind a façade of proper conduct or well-mannered behavior, which seems flat or ingenuine as it splits off the painful and shadowy land of shame. Indeed in my daily practice shame does not freely uncover itself. At the most, patients tend to complain about situations that make them feel insufficient or self-reproaching, but they do not consciously or openly link such feelings with shame. Some do not even dare so much self-disclosure, but remain hidden behind shallow collective attributions, with allusions to the ridiculousness of their condition, e.g.: "Shouldn't I feel different, overcome my true feelings? I *should* be happy but why can't I feel it?" Taking sides with the deprecating gaze of their peers, these patients can appear to lack the capacity to confront their own inner truth.

Manifestations of shame have accompanied analytical efforts from the beginning. Expressions of shame have been often unjustly interpreted as resistance, lack of differentiation, unreachability, or defiance—all indicating that the patient is to blame, and thus extending the problem instead of addressing/attending to it. Shame is located at the edge between Self and Other, and at the same time it resides in the core of a person's fragile being. Therefore a prerequisite for healing is the real or assumed glance of a meaningful Other which is closely connected to the subtle activation of the archetype of relationship. The in-between location of shame makes it highly contagious, which can explain its silencing impact on the analyst, such as when he or she becomes overwhelmed by countertransference feelings like fatigue or dullness. Thus looking at shame from a Jungian perspective brings us close to the findings of object relations theory and intersubjectivity, which also stress the importance of early relationship, and transference and countertransference. Working with shame in analysis, we deal with the upsetting but often hidden reality of traumatic and mortifying events that occurred in close and early relationships. Such experiences rupture the individual's psychic continuity, and lead toward a dissociative blockage of emotional processing. This disruptive process entails at least a partial arrest of psychic development, which causes, among other things, significant obstacles to affective communication.

Neurobiologically viewed, those hidden blocks redirect implicit and nonverbal layers of affective communication straight toward a mind–body metabolic collapse and thereby toward a loss of energy-dependent synaptic connectivity within the right brain. The end outcome is a sudden implosion of the implicit self and a rupture of self-continuity. Equally bad, according to Margaret Wilkinson, one of the outstanding Jungians who works in the field of early trauma, shame can be understood as overwhelming passive hostility against the Self, which can put the therapeutic relationship as a whole on trial. Research has found proof that the right brain is "online" from birth, that it is relational and implicit, and that it thus plays a key role in early emotional learning processes. Furthermore early right-hemisphere activity stimulates the growth of the speech and language centers in the later developing left hemisphere. In forming new relationships, older children continue to mirror ways of being with others, a process that builds on their already firmly established inner expectations. So, when a mother or meaningful Other repeatedly fails to respond in a related way, the world becomes a terrifying place. Ultimately the consequence of this wounding is psychic fragmentation and the deprivation of rootedness in meaning-making. According to Wilkinson,

> When the rupture in attachment caused by shaming has been frequent, prolonged and unmitigated by experiences of repair, the neuronal pathways for self-hate and fear of the other become strongly established and the other becomes a source of terror and dread rather than a source of supportive relationship.[10]

Freudian analyst Leon Wurmser comes to a similar conclusion in his almost poetic and at the same time highly evocative book, *The Mask of Shame*:

> Shame at its deepest layer is the conviction of one's unlovability, an inherent sense that the self is dirty, untouchable, rotten … this abyss of unlovability contains such a depth of wordless and imageless despair that any more delimited shame comes as a welcome friend—its visibility and concreteness protect against the gray ghost of that absolute shame.… To be unlovable means not to see a responsive eye and not to hear a responding voice …. [T]he helplessness of the searching eye and of the cry is the helplessness of feeling doomed to unlovability.[11]

Other well-known colleagues connected with the understanding of shame are the Jungians Mario Jacoby, Ursula Wirtz, Mary Ayers, and Jean Knox. Among the Freudians, I want to recall Anna Freud, Donald Winnicott, Heinz Kohut, John Bowlby, and Daniel Stern. All of these analysts have contributed with both their theoretical findings and their willingness to share moving episodes from their work with clients.

Mary Ayers especially stresses the impact of early trauma inflicted by "the eyes of the contemptuous, unreflecting, or still mother's face;" from preverbal stages onward, she emphasizes, this results in forsaken loneliness, in a freezing, petrifying shame.[12] Here Ayers refers to the transformational Greek myth of the Gorgo Medusa, the once beautiful young girl, said to have been raped by Poseidon in Athena's temple. To summarize the development:

> After the rape, the motherless goddess Athena curses the girl, causing her to take the shape of the monstrous deadly creature, Medusa. Instead of hair, venomous snakes grow from her head, and she turns to stone all who dare to gaze on her dreadful face. With Athena's advice Perseus beheads the Medusa by looking

at her reflection in his shield, thus avoiding a direct view of her horrible grimace. The already pregnant Medusa, upon her death, gives birth to twins. Finally, Athena receives Medusa's head and mounts it on her shield as a special protective charm.

In my understanding, it is only in the *aftermath* of trauma that the dreadful, mutilated, and desperately one-sided, archetypal Terrible Mother fully emerges, that is, when Medusa's original trauma (symbolized by the rape) is met with an outright deprivation of feminine solidarity (symbolized in Athena's curse). Transcending the historical bias of gender role in the ancient Greek world—and not to get trapped in a perhaps instinctual feminine solidarity with victims of trauma—the initially animus-possessed Athena suggests a fundamental absence of feminine empathy occurring specifically in a society or other collective that is one-sidedly dominated by the masculine principle.

My deep compassion lies with Medusa's complex, demonic drivenness and her bi-directional suffering, for she is both punished and punishing until Athena finally and equitably redeems her as a protective power. As Ayers explains, the petrifying glance of the wounded Great (Evil) Mother, humanly embodied, suppresses the emergence of the child's creativity. This is because creativity, opening the way to new life, would risk the death of that which is familiar and sustaining if also harmful to both mother and child—namely the mortifying mother/child bond. Keeping this dynamic in mind is helpful for finding non-judgmental access to the paralyzed state that might manifest itself in a patient's vague complaints of boredom, disinterest, fatigue, and/or endless and haunting reproaches to the analyst. Ayers stresses that all kinds of trauma, especially early relational traumata, have their onset in a "crack" or a series of cracks in the flow of emotional development. That's why she points out that a reversal of the crack needs elaborate, sometimes insisting and wide exploration of the slightest gaps in emotional perception.

At this point I would like to share some of my practical experience that has been encouraged by my reading of the French Freudian analyst Caroline Eliacheff. For almost thirty years she worked as a consultant in a maternity hospital with women who came from difficult social backgrounds, and who struggled with the decision to put their babies up for adoption. Working with those highly ambivalent or even rejecting women, Eliacheff was increasingly asked to attend to the newborns who were in life-threatening situations. She collected the babies' biographical backgrounds and then, *to contain the distressed atmosphere*, she tried to attune to their petrified, monotonous cries of abandonment. Then she very calmly processed back to each baby what she had learned about his or her life, mostly referring to the emotional climate. She sometimes responded using merely the melody of her voice; other times she actually verbalized the situation. As she tuned into the emotions, witnessed the baby's mostly unsuccessful struggle to get in touch with the mother, and resonated with the boundless grief and desperation, Eliacheff realized the benefits of the process: The muscular tension of her little patients decreased, many of them fell into a calm sleep, and they seemed to fully recover within days. In my own practice, I too attended to newborns, even premature infants. Inspired by Eliacheff, I too retold and reframed their stories, explaining that they were experiencing the shock of emotional overload due to their early exposure to threatening environments or to surroundings that were otherwise non-welcoming or not sufficiently coping. Repeatedly the mothers and I witnessed an unbelievable relaxation in their infants (and in the mothers themselves, whom I usually sensed as being desperately unable to cope). Ever since, I have been encouraging young parents to dare to address difficult emotional issues with an authentic and containing attitude, even with their small children.

In contrast to guilt, shame lacks the somewhat hopeful potential of ambivalence. The victim of shame is one-sidedly forced to helpless inactivity, is put completely and utterly at the mercy of others—and this, due to the underlying neurobiological process of partial parasympathetic collapse. The threat of psychic death—which, in rare cases, can even spread to somatic death—is a one-dimensional experience. It is sealed off by the defenses of silence and other mechanisms that aim at self-invisibility, because to be witnessed in shame is to bear all the more shame (whereas other painful states can be reduced or improved by the experience of being seen). Shame alienates us from meaningful Others; it is the most secretive and hidden prison one can think of. Furthermore shame deprives us of the capacity to regulate and modulate our emotions; it sentences an individual to a standstill, as if with no prospect of redemption. The explanations, justifications, and pleas of caring Others cannot be heard or taken into account. Masochistic self-judgment, another outgrowth of shame, is ruthless and cruel beyond reach. It brings self-disgust and pervading self-loathing, which infiltrate from the inside, deepening one's own self-alienation and fragmenting introspection.

Thus it is of utmost importance for the therapist to patiently assume the role of the "unbribable wailers," as we know them from the Sumerian myth of Inanna and Ereshkigal. Two small characters, made of earth, embody the virtues of empathy, creative fertility, and mirroring resonance and, by unwavering witnessing, release the sufferer's sorrow, lament, and, finally, redemption. A similar function can be found in popular practices centered on the pious Blessed Mother Mary. Even more so, we find it in the Buddhist *bodhisattva Avalokitesvara*—"the regarder of the cries of the world" or "the perceiver of sounds." *Avalokitesvara* is the enlightened being whose attributes include gentleness, responsiveness, empathy, and other helpful qualities—the variety of which point to *Avalokitesvara's* message that compassion manifests itself in any form that might benefit the supplicant.

In contrast to shame, guilt can be understood as one's inherent sense or realization of having done wrong. Not necessarily evoked by other people, guilt can be felt within as one's own moral or ethical sense. Shame, on the other hand, is something foreign and inseparably bound to the real or suspected accusing gaze of others—and it isolates the sufferer in nameless mists of loneliness or even invisibility.

The previously mentioned Leon Wurmser and our deceased colleague Mario Jacoby shed light on another level of understanding shame, a dimension that goes under the rubric of, "a guardian of human dignity." In contrast to what we might call "degrading shame," this dignity-preserving shame embodies a heightened awareness of the innate right for one's self and others to be valued with emotional and ethical fairness. Translated to the dynamic process of coming to terms with one's personal biography, the energy load of early shame can be perceived positively as the moving force that safeguards the inner potential of the Self. In other words, with transformed perception, the very shame that secludes can be valued as that which guards our highest inner ideals and protects them from destruction by both outside influences and introjects. In this approach, Medusa's redemption by Athena—the conversion of her petrifying gaze into a protective force—alludes to this transformation in service of the sanctuary of the Self. Thus the subtle instant when a shamed individual can turn his or her mercy towards themselves can be witnessed as the momentum of psychic re-birth. In specifically Jungian terms then, "purified" shame can serve to maintain loyalty toward the Self and the inner call of individuation. Freudian analyst Benjamin Kilborne alludes to this call when he notes that, "to hide one's despair from oneself is to waste one's life."[13]

I would now like to mention the impact of the transgenerational, inherited shame that regularly occurs in collective situations of war, displacement, and concomitant exposure to violence. In our society in general we perceive a growing awareness of individual trauma, especially in connection with early abandonment and neglect, violence, and sexual abuse. Looking back at almost sixty years of constant peace in central Europe, one might (light-mindedly) expect that we have come to terms with collective trauma. Actually psyche teaches a different lesson, for only recently has a wider public begun to realize the destructive consequences of the voiceless shame that future generations inherited from World War II. In addition, migrants and refugees from many countries across the world are now relocating in Europe from places where collectives are repressed and threats to their lives persist.

Thus in my practice in Germany, both Germans and foreigners present an ongoing, collective trend of emotional depletion and voicelessness, which I understand partly as a generation-overlapping phenomenon linked to war damage. Past suffering affects not only those directly afflicted. Rather, it proliferates through the generations, due to the persisting shock of the foregoing generation(s) and the paralysis of their ability to heal and provide emotional containment for others. For instance in today's Germany, many grandchildren and great-grandchildren, now adults, still carry the burden of muteness, numbness, and fragmentation inherited from World War II. Many of them struggle to overcome the ramifications of collective shame, of which they are increasingly less aware because of the distance of time and/or the lack of direct involvement and of betrayed narrative tradition. And this, despite the fact that, by now, numerous publications give autobiographical evidence, bear witness to the sustained atrocities and injustices, and testify to the almost crippling impact of impoverished emotional resonance. At any rate, the hiding and disguising of the background shame are still at stake.

Along the consequences are a diminished ability to feel empathy—and sometimes the sufferers even present an outspoken lack of capacity to register any sense of shame whatsoever.

Emotionally torn to pieces, many patients with such histories still lack a larger, transgenerational narrative that can explain the greater background of their shame, their multiple experiences of abandonment within close private circles, and the overwhelming of all but their shallowest capacity to adapt. These individuals may find themselves in a vicious circle that manifests itself as an inherited blunting of the ability to feel empathy, accompanied by the tendencies to feel exposed and unprotected, and more explicitly, to compulsively re-enact early negative encounters that are stored in the depths of their inner abysses. They lack healthy coping strategies for interpersonal relationships. Sometimes, more tragically, they are unable to even let go, to genuinely enter into any relationship at all. Many of them experienced early rejection, shame, and withdrawal as the sole basis of relating, meaning that relationship as such (or nearly any prospect of it) triggers the same feelings. So, in order to cope, the sufferers might resort to repetitive identification with the aggressor, reenacting the background of appeasement of both the aggressor and themselves by numbing their cognitive abilities and/or aggressively acting out their despair. In other words, many of these patients have little or no ability to mentalize, that is, to imaginatively grasp the mental state of oneself and others—a faculty that ordinarily underlies our overt behavior. Peter Fonagy and Margret Target, renowned London-based researchers in this area, assume that by the age of four or five, children should have a sound capacity to reflect on inner states and find ways to deal with discrepancies between the inner and outer worlds. This competency is severely blocked by shame, which, coming from and triggering further blockages of energy, results in a future that severely lacks empathy.

What impact do all these reflections have on analysis? How does an individual quest for a meaningful life finally emerge? How can inner growth and healing be facilitated? Or, to follow Jung's "essential question,"

> [W]hat will pierce through this fog of verbiage to the conscious personality of the patient, and what must be the nature of his

> attitude if he is to integrate that split-off fragment, supposing it
> were ever part of him? … Something, therefore, that belongs to
> him in the deepest sense, completes him, creates organic balance,
> and yet for some reason is feared, perhaps because it makes life
> complicated and sets apparently impossible tasks?[14]

The main idea I want to unfold is that of the earlier mentioned link
of shame to dignity. I take it that, in Jungian terms, "dignity" can be
defined as a deeply-felt sense of wholeness, which in this context would
include an accepting and letting go of degrading shame, and finally
coming to terms with suffering and death. It is the growing awareness
of the on-going process of individuation—which, as Jung observes, "is
a heroic and often tragic task, [and as] the most difficult [task] of all,
it involves suffering …"[15]

Shame blocks the continuity of life and psychic experience, as does
trauma. As shame mostly does not allow our recollections of a "before"
and "after," it can be at one and the same time both shattering and
creeping. Very often, like a slow-working venom, shame undermines
our trust in others and in our own coping strategies—as does trauma.
Life-sustaining values and attitudes get shattered and destroyed.
Unresolved shame reduces the likelihood of developing meaningful
relationships, which in turn reduces the likelihood of using empathy
to outgrow unsettling shame. Instead, suspiciousness leads to
withdrawal from meaningful others, to depleted emotional
attunement, and to a severe loss of vitality. Sometimes it might be
helpful to explain these mechanisms to patients.

Now, what is the basic attitude needed in a professional,
therapeutic approach with people trapped in the shame of betrayal,
injury, and injustice, or exposure to brute violence? How can we
responsibly encourage individuation processes? The symbol that might
very fundamentally describe the required attitude is that of the
alchemical *vas*, i.e. the therapeutic container or frame that creates a
unique space of growth and attendance to soul. The containing ground
is offered in the therapist's provision of a secure environment, which
in part entails one's unconditional acceptance of the patient's inner
truth—be it somatic, psychic, or imagined. An essential and long-
standing part of the practical framework consists of the therapist and
patient sharing in a mutually growing awareness of and differentiation
between inner and outer reality, the fluidity of past versus present
experience, and varying ego states. Thus it is crucial for the therapist

to develop an inner stance of tact and the courage to look at the shadow realm of prejudices and the way those prejudices contribute to a patient's speechlessness or unrelatedness. One's asking for analysis per se can be credited, at the very least, as an acknowledgement of need.

Still, it is not uncommon at the start of therapy for patients to (unconsciously) disguise their most vulnerable psychic spots. For instance, they might be convinced that their suffering lies only in somatic symptoms combined with the blankness of depression. Yet many somatoform disorders, pain syndromes—and notably fibromyalgia—are known to be intimately related to shame and trauma. Many trauma victims end up with chronic fatigue, which results from the constant firing of the sympathetic nervous system, a burning out of the adrenal glands, and finally a trap where neither fight nor flight are options anymore and psychological paralysis prevails. Other places to be on the lookout for hidden signs of shame: with elderly patients who present cognitive deficits; with severely somatically ill patients; and as well, with patients who present all kinds of social distress.

The signs and symptoms call for on-going differentiation between the threat of negative introjects on one hand, and on the other hand, the impulse to grow and to integrate forlorn and rebellious fragments of the soul. For both parties—i.e. for the therapist and the patient— it can be exhausting to fight firmly against the cruelty of harmful introjects while at the same time trying to uncover the authentic vital forces that seem buried under the loads of shame. Reliable hints of progress can register as subtle shifts of emotion and somatic responses in one's countertransference, and as well, in repeating signs of an unconscious alliance between patient and analyst. The patient's inner development expresses itself as a cautious process, whereby introjected negative attributes gradually become ego-dystonic. As many early experiences of shame are mediated by the nonverbal right brain hemisphere, it is important to be open to the support available in the variety of nonverbal self-care disciplines, such as those offered in yoga, tai chi, qi gong, the arts therapies, and mindfulness-based stress reduction (MBSR).

Given that the fragments of every single biography add to a morphogenetic field that continuously creates itself, what can finally emerge from the experience of entrenched, degrading shame is a new vision of a meaningful life. Even those unresolvable issues that have become constituent elements of a person's self-image deserve to be lived in dignity, with a containing sense of meaning.

* * *

I would like to finish with a scene from the original, 1812 German version of the Grimm's, "The Maiden Without Hands." One of the outstanding fairy tales interpreted in the context of sexual abuse, it speaks as well to other circumstances of deep humiliation. Regardless of the version, the plot centers on the maiden whose father chopped off her hands due to his bargain with the devil. Throughout most of the story, the maiden remains unable to actively deal with her fate. She merely survives by feeding herself and her son, but never opposes any hardship laid upon her. The original version points to a most deep and hidden process that develops unconditional compassion, trust, healing, and the victim's courage to re-enter life. I have been unable to find a corresponding English translation, thus I retell it here:

> Finally, after her long and painful quest, and looking desperately for shelter in a huge forest, the maiden came upon a good old man sitting next to a well. "Be so merciful," she said, "and hold my child at your breast until I have given him enough to drink." The old man thought awhile, and then said to her, "Over there stands a big, stout tree. Go and wrap your stumped arms around it three times!" And when she did this, her hands grew back. Then the old man showed her a house. "Go and live there, and don't go out, and don't open the door for anyone who doesn't plead three times to enter by God's will."[16]

NOTES

[1] Cited in Benjamin Kilborne, *Disappearing Persons* (Albany: State University of New York Press, 2002), p. 6.

[2] *The Holy Bible*, Genesis 3:10, King James Version (Philadelphia: National Publishing Company, 1978).

[3] *Ibid.*, Isaiah, 54:4.

[4] William Shakespeare, *Julius Caesar* (Dortmund: Verlag Lambert Lensing, 1958), Act II, Scene 2.

⁵ Jane Austen, *Pride and Prejudice* (London: The Penguin English Library, 1979), pp. 236-237.

⁶ Joseph Conrad, *Lord Jim: A Tale* (London: Penguin Modern Classics, 1977), pp. 307-313.

⁷ C.G. Jung, "The Transcendent Function," *The Structure and Dynamics of the Psyche*, Vol. 8, § 169-170, *The Collected Works*, eds. Sir Herbert Read, Michael Fordham, Gerhard Adler, William McGuire, trans. R.F.C. Hull, Bollingen Series XX, Fifth Printing (Princeton: Princeton University Press, 1981). All future references to the *Collected Works*, abbreviated to CW, will be followed by chapter title and volume and paragraph numbers.

⁸ Donald Kalsched, *Trauma and the Soul: A Psycho-Spiritual Approach to Human Development and Its Interruption* (London: Routledge, 2013), p. 4.

⁹ Leon Wurmser, *The Mask of Shame* (Baltimore, MD: Johns Hopkins University Press, 1997).

¹⁰ Margaret Wilkinson, *Changing Minds in Therapy: Emotion, Attachment, Trauma, and Neurobiology*, Norton Series on Interpersonal Neurobiology (New York: Norton & Company, 2010), p. 110.

¹¹ Wurmser, *The Mask of Shame*, pp. 96-97.

¹² Mary Y. Ayers, *Mother-Infant Attachment and Psychoanalysis: The Eyes of Shame* (Hove, Sussex: Brunner-Routledge, 2003), p. 216.

¹³ Kilborne, *Disappearing Persons*, p. 89.

¹⁴ Jung, "The State of Psychotherapy Today," CW 10, § 364.

¹⁵ *Ibid.*, "A Psychological Approach to the Trinity," CW 11, § 233.

¹⁶ "Das Mädchen ohne Hände," in Brüder Grimm, *Kinder- und Hausmärchen*, Erstdruckfassung 1812-1815 (Eschborn: Verlag Dietmar Klotz, 2004), No. 31, my summary from the original German (1812).

6

On the Role of Failure in the Individuation Process

Murray Stein

INTRODUCTION

I have to confess that I had a difficult time getting into this Odyssey theme, "the crucible of failure." Partly this was due to a resistance I felt to this painful subject; perhaps it is even due to a "failure complex" on my part. I examined myself and of course found that this is regretably true. It was also because of a fear of failing at such an important topic for psychology and psychotherapy, a fear of speaking only banalities and half-baked superficialities that take up a generously allotted time but do not bring much new insight. Plus, seeing that my lecture was scheduled at the end of this odyssey into failure and imagining that the audience would be sick and tired of thinking and hearing about failure for a whole week—and besides will have heard from other speakers most everything smart that can be said on the subject already, will have considered all the angles and arrived at considered solutions—well, that gave me a lot of anxiety too. Who wants to fail on the subject of failure? Not a pleasant prospect. But if one should succeed at talking about failure, would this not be a failure of another kind? Isn't it a paradox to succeed at speaking about failure and feel it's been a success? But who wants to demonstrate failure in front of a distinguished audience? So many questions.

On top of that, I also had to figure out what the assignment given in the Odyssey theme for this year actually was. More problems. What does "The Crucible of Failure" mean? This did not strike me as self-evident and transparent. Is "failure" to be taken as itself being the "crucible"? In other words, is the experience of failure itself the container in which the experience of "failure" cooks, like sitting in the depths of darkness in the *nigredo* and waiting for "failure" to transform into something else from out of itself, like a phoenix rising from its ashes? Or is "failure" something to put into an external "crucible" and there cook, melt down, transform? If so, then what is the "crucible," the melting pot, the container in which failure can be transformed?

The question for me was this: are these two terms separable, or are they to be merged into one and the same thing? If failure is the crucible, what happens when it is melted by itself, into itself? Its specificity and identity seem to be so unitary as it is. It does not seem to have energy to be able to move itself. Left by itself and in itself, would it not just intensify the reality of failure and distill it into a solid essence? Would it not become a rock in the stomach, an intractable complex that is carried to the grave, and perhaps beyond, like karma?

I was led to the thought that failure cannot be the crucible for its own transformation. Maybe this is the Christian element in my mind, which says that we cannot save ourselves, that we need another, grace from above, from outside. The failed ego cannot change itself. It needs a crucible, and the crucible must be a container somewhat separate from the failure-ego. This is a necessary condition for failure's transformation. Failure, whether a subjective feeling state (a failure-ego) or an objective event (an experiment, for instance), needs to be placed into a context (a crucible) bigger than itself and its own narrowly limited horizon—for failure constructs an extremely small horizon of visibility—and then perhaps it can be brought into a perspective that recognizes failure as a part of the much greater on-going opus (an individuation process that encompasses all of a lifetime or scientific discovery as a total human endeavor).

In this discussion, I want to consider primarily the place of the experience of failure, the recognition of failure, and deep-seated feelings of failure in life in the light of the individuation process and its cycles of expansion of consciousness, which move toward the recognition of the self at work in the individual's life. At the conclusion, I will also consider collective and global human failures in this perspective.

So, putting aside my fears and questions and deciding that failure is not the crucible and the crucible is not failure, I took some faltering steps forward. In the course of time, various bits of information and items fell into my lap, synchronistically, which I could use to patch together some reflections on "the role of failure in the individuation process." In what follows, I hope to suggest a state of equilibrium between the opposites success-and-failure in the individuation process.

The essay is in three parts: crucible, failure, and transformation.

THE CRUCIBLE

So let's begin by considering the "crucible." First, what is the meaning of the term "crucible" and what is the history of this unusual and rarely used English word? Etymology lends depth to our grasp of language. We must know what we are talking about when we use such potent and suggestive words. Here, from *The Oxford Dictionary of English Etymology*:

> crucible: vessel for fusing metals. Xv (early forms *corusible*, *kressibule*). –medL. *Crucibulum* night-lamp, crucible, f.L. *cruc-*, *crux* CROSS; perh. Orig. lamp hanging before a crucifix.

With this definition of "crucible" as a vessel for fusing metals we find ourselves engaged with a metallurgical metaphor and, for us even more important, with an alchemical one. We may think of the crucible as a *vas mirabile*, the alchemical vessel of transformation, about which Jung writes:

> Maria Prophetissa says that the whole secret lies in knowing about the Hermetic vessel. "Unum est vas" (the vessel is one) is emphasized again and again... One naturally thinks of this vessel as a sort of retort or flask; but one soon learns that this is an inadequate conception since the vessel is more a mystical idea, a true symbol like all the central ideas of alchemy. Thus we hear

that the vas is the water or *aqua permanens*, which is none other
than the Mercurius of the philosophers.[1]

From this passage we learn that the *vas mirabile* is a symbol. The
alchemists were not speaking of mere pots and pans. They dealt in
symbols. The *vas mirabile* is a miraculous container whose meaning
extends out into an endless number of directions. Basically, it is the
means and the psychic location of transformation. We can think of it
as sacred space with strong hermeneutical properties. That is, a
protected psychic space where Mercurius, the energy of transformation,
is present and active.

The etymology of the English word *crucible* sets us forth in a
similar direction by linking the vessel for fusing metals to *crux*, the
cross, a classic symbolic holder of "failure," and reminding us of
the Biblical passage:

> When it was noon, darkness came over the whole land until
> three in the afternoon. At three o'clock Jesus cried out with a
> loud voice, "Eloi, Eloi, lema sabachthani?" which means, "My
> God, my God, why have you forsaken me?"[2]

The cross marks the anguished space of failure, and the locus of its
transformation. *Crucibilum*, from which our word crucible comes,
designates a night-lamp, perhaps originally hanging in front of a
cross in a church or cathedral, so casts a light on the moment of
Jesus' "failure" as a secular messiah and his transformation into a
spiritual savior.

The cross is the crucible on which failure was transformed into
triumph, a potent symbol of transformation therefore, where failure
was melted down and converted into a meaning that combines the
opposites failure/success into a formulation that leads to a new level
of consciousness, a symbolic and spiritual level. The failed Jesus of
history became interpreted for his followers and transformed, then and
to this day, into the living Christ who unites in himself the human
and the divine and is a living symbol of Divine Love precisely because
of his wounds, the marks of his earthly failure.

So we come to the understanding that the "crucible" is a
psychically potent symbolic instrument that has the capacity to
transform failure into something quite different from what appearances
alone would suggest on their mundane level.

For the purpose of reflection on the theme for this year's Jungian Odyssey, let's consider that analysis may be a modern crucible for melting down the feeling and strong awareness of failure in life and transforming it; that analysis may be a symbolic container where the feeling and judgment of *failure* can be transformed into a critical moment, even a pivot point, in the narrative of the self's incarnation in a person's life, i.e., individuation. Analysis may be "the vessel for fusing metals," as the definition of "crucible" puts is, and more than that, for transforming them in the alchemical fashion.

I say, "may be," because I do not want to set Jungian psychoanalysis and psychotherapy up for inevitable failure in delivering on overblown promises. We who practice the art of this modern mode in the "care of souls" know that not every case is a story of transformation, and that we are often enough called upon to put our sense of failure as analysts into the crucible for transformation. But we also know that sometimes the transformation does happen within the context of the therapeutic relationship. Most often we do not know why this comes about, and Jungians tend to attribute the "crucible effect," to give it a name, to the spontaneous workings of the unconscious out of whose creative womb a symbol emerges that has the transforming effect. There are many testimonials to this, and I will cite one that appeared recently in the pages of the *Financial Times*, in an article by the psychologically astute columnist Harry Eyers:

> I go with the great Chilean pianist Claudio Arrau who as a despairing young man, contemplating suicide, found his salvation in Jungian psychoanalysis. He felt increasingly liberated from physical, emotional and psychological blocks and able to express himself as an artist and as a man. As Arrau wrote of Mahler: "Anguish and fear of death had given way to a firm belief in the indestructibility of the human soul."[3]

I do not know the details of Claudio Arrau's biography (1903-1991), but I imagine he felt himself to be a hopeless failure at that time in his life when he entered the crucible of Jungian analysis. So the transformation was critical and resulted in many years of masterful performances in concert halls worldwide. In a brief biography online, we find the following tribute to Arrau's artistry:

> Where other famous pianists play the piano for excitement,
> power or display, Arrau plays to probe, to divine, to interpret.
> Says Arrau, "An interpreter must give his blood to the work
> interpreted." The famed late doyen of London music critics, Sir
> Neville Cardus of the Guardian, explained Arrau vividly: "Arrau
> is the complete pianist. He can revel in the keyboard for its own
> pianistic sake, representing to us the instrument's range and
> power, but he can also go beyond piano playing as we are led by
> his art to the secret chambers of the creative imagination."[4]

It may well be that Arrau's capacity to enter and explore "the secret
chambers of the creative imagination" came into being as a result of a
transformation in the crucible of analysis.

"FAILURE"

Let's turn now to "failure," the other term in our theme for this
year's Jungian Odyssey. How should we think about this dire topic?
How shall we define it? *The Oxford Dictionary of English Etymology* offers
us a surprisingly psychological suggestion:

> failure: default; want of success. fail: be wanting or
> insufficient; lose power, fail or come short, be in default. XIII.
> – (O)F. *faillir* be wanting – Pr. *falhir* :_ Rom. *fallire*, from L.
> *fallere* deceive and used in the sense 'disappoint expectation,
> be wanting or defective.'

The source of the English word is rooted in the Latin *fallere*, to
deceive. When we think we perceive something and are deceived;
when we hope for something and are disappointed; when we project
our wishes and desires and become disillusioned after we discover
that the objects or objectives upon which we had placed our psychic
images of great expectation are "wanting or defective"—we then
experience "failure." From this it becomes obvious that, as
inherently psychological beings, we are destined to feelings of
failure because desire, ambition, projection, expectation, and hope
are rooted in our psychic nature.

So let's say that we may experience failure in any one or all of the
following instances: a) when we fail ourselves (falling short of high
expectations for ourselves that are rooted in our personal ego-driven
ambitions); b) when other people or things fail us (they fall short of

expectations rooted in our unconscious projections and desires); c) when we fail others (we fall short of expectations rooted in our narcissistic self-image). Failure is the feeling and the judgment of default, insufficiency, loss of power over our world and ourselves. Failure is a defeat for the ego and its narcissistic self-image.

Success, failure's opposite, is the perfect set-up for failure. Success increases expectations of self and others, so the greater the success the more dramatic the failure. The price of fame is failure. This truism cannot be reversed without exception: the reward for failure is not inevitably success, although it can happen. Jung was leery of worldly success, of which he had much, and so would say upon returning home from a hugely applauded trip to foreign lands, to America for instance, when asked how it was: "Well, I've suffered another success!" He was prepared for the boomerang effect.

Once we start looking carefully at "failure" as a psychological experience, we soon enough realize that failure is inevitable and ubiquitous. Everybody fails and at times feels like a failure. This can easily turn into a cliché, of course, but it is still painful and valid. We are born into failure—to always imperfect and often quite unconscious young mothers; into dysfunctional and sometimes horribly abusive families; into one-sided and failing or already failed societies and cultures. Moreover, we continually create new failures, individually and collectively. We suffer from feelings of failure in one degree or another every day of our lives. You don't have to believe in "original sin" to realize that human beings are fatally set up to fail and to experience failure. It is empirical. It is the human condition. The question is, what do we do with our failures—as individuals and societies? If we cannot change the fundamental features of our nature that lead invariably to failure, can we use failure to become more conscious? Is consciousness of failure, indeed, the necessary pre-condition for later success and progress? Does failure have an essential function in the individuation process? If so, what is it?

One major cause of people's failures in life and especially at interpersonal relationships (as well as in cultural exchanges and political relationships) is what Jung called "psychological type," and has become more popularly known as "personality type." We inherit a basic proclivity to run to psychological type and we inevitably do so to a lesser or greater extreme, so that in the course of development, both individually and collectively, typology becomes exaggerated and one-sided. This is deeply rooted in the nature of human psychological development. Perhaps the steepness of the gradient that leads to the one-sidedness of type can be attributed to laziness: We don't want to be bothered by what we don't do well or easily, by what fatigues and frustrates us, so we proceed blithely on the easier path of following the gradient of our superior functions. When we operate from our preferred or superior functions only, however, we run into all kinds of failures—to ourselves, to others, and to our self-esteem. We are humiliated and defeated by ourselves and by the world around because of our failure in achieving typological wholeness.

In effect, psychological type contributes importantly to character, and, as Freud said so pithily, character is destiny.

TRANSFORMATION—REVERSING THE PERSPECTIVE

So now to the crucial question: Is it possible to transform the feeling and experience of failure in a crucible and thereby turn it into something of value for individuation? Is it perhaps meaningful that we as psychological beings are doomed to feelings of failure?

Let's consider this pregnant statement by Jung:

> The self, in its efforts at self-realization, reaches out beyond the ego-personality on all sides; because of its all-encompassing nature it is brighter and darker than the ego, and accordingly confronts it with problems which it would like to avoid. Either one's moral courage fails, or one's insight, or both, until in the end fate decides. The ego never lacks moral and rational counterarguments, which one cannot and should not set aside so long as it is possible to hold on to them. For you only feel yourself on the right road when the conflicts of duty seem to have resolved themselves, and you have become the victim of a decision made over your head or in defiance of the heart. From this we can see the numinous power of the self, which can hardly be experienced in any other way. For this reason *the experience of the self is always a defeat for the ego.*[5]

Is the opposite also the case? Is the defeat of the ego's will to power and success potentially (always!) an experience of the self? Does failure carry a message from the self—like a dream? This will occupy our attention for the remainder of this essay.

We are speaking of failure as an aspect of the individuation process. As a reminder, a short definition of individuation would be the gradual incarnation of the self in an individual's life experience over the course of an entire lifetime. This means that the individuating person attains to greater consciousness of the self in this process and to an extent is released from the narrow precincts of the ego and the complexes that determine its emotional reactions. In the definition of failure, we saw that it depends on psychological dynamics and factors such as projection and grandiosity. These become problems for the ego because they lead to illusory expectations for oneself and of others, including non-human others even like nature itself. People are disappointed and depressed because they get old and decrepit, for instance. Nature has let them down and they are disappointed. Nature has failed them. Or we may see ourselves as failures because the financial world collapses and we weren't clever enough to anticipate such a development or find a broker who could guide us to a safe harbor. We may consider ourselves failures as children of our expectant parents, and we may judge ourselves to be failures as parents because our children disappoint us. All of these are defeats for the ego and are therefore judged as failures. Failure is a judgment of the ego, either against itself or another. But when the ego's will is defeated, is the self teaching us something in these failures? Are we individuating with and through failure against our wills, willy-nilly and in spite of ourselves? Do these experiences of failure offer us a glimpse of the self at work and incarnating in our seemingly failed lives?

Here is Jung's tip from his studies of alchemy:

> The Golden Fleece is the coveted goal of the argosy, the perilous quest that is one of the numerous synonyms for attaining the unattainable. Thales makes this wise remark about it:
>
>> That is indeed what men most seek on earth:
>> 'Tis rust alone that gives the coin its worth!
>
> ... . In the alchemical view rust, like verdigris, is the metal's sickness. But at the same time this leprosy is the *vera prima materia*, the basis for the preparation of the philosophical gold. The *Rosarium* says:
>
>> Our gold is not the common gold. But thou hast inquired concerning the greenness [*viriditas*, presumably verdigris], deeming the bronze to be a

leprous body on account of the greenness it hath upon
it. Therefore I say unto thee that whatever is perfect
in the bronze is that greenness only, because that
greenness is straightway changed by our magistery into
our most true gold. [Followed by Jung's footnote
number 73.]

[Footnote 73:] *Art. aurif.*, II, p. 220: a quotation from Senior.
Viriditas is occasionally called *Azoth*, which is one of the
numerous synonyms for the stone.

The paradoxical remark of Thales that the rust alone gives the
coin its true value is a kind of alchemical quip, which at bottom
only says that there is no light without shadow and no psychic
wholeness without imperfection. To round itself out, life calls
not for perfection but for completeness; and for this the "thorn
in the flesh" is needed, the suffering of defects without which
there is no progress and no ascent.[6]

These lines are packed with ideas that provoke thought and
reflection, and I don't want to hurry by them. First, let's consider
vera prima materia and Azoth. The rust or greenness of the metal,
which is the metal's imperfection—the metal's "failure" in the sense
of not living up to expectations, imperfect, disappointing, a default
in nature—is equated to *vera prima materia* and Azoth. This failure
of the metal's capacity to maintain its state of perfection "gives the
coin its worth." A paradox. The alchemists have reversed
perspective. Can we follow them?

We know that alchemy's transformative magic is impossible to
activate in the absence of essential material to work with, the *vera prima
materia* (the real stuff, the archetypal matter). This is what the recipes
were all about—how to collect *prima materia* and cook it in the crucible.
The crucible needs *prima materia* before the work can begin. The text
says you can find it in the rust, in the metal's failure. This is where to
look for the stuff that will in the end yield alchemical "gold" and
constellate the presence of the *filius philosophorum*. In psychological
language, this "material" is what brings individuation into the realm
of possibility and leads to the realization of the self. The *prima materia*
is in "the rust," the "greenness" of the bronze, the "leprous body." This
Viriditas is sometimes called *Azoth*.

So who, or what, is *Azoth*?

> Azoth is the essential agent of transformation in alchemy. It is
> the name given by ancient alchemists to Mercury, the animating
> spirit hidden in all matter that makes transmutation possible.
> The spelling consists of the initial letter of the English, Greek
> and Hebrew alphabets followed by the final letters of the English
> alphabet (Z), the Greek alphabet (Omega) and the Hebrew
> alphabet (Tau). The word comes from the Arabic *al-zāʾbūq*
> which means "Mercury." The word occurs in the writings of
> many early alchemists, such as Zosimos, Mary the Jewess,
> Olympiodorus, and Jābir ibn Hayyān (Geber).[7]

Mercurius is embedded in the "greenness," i.e., in the failure of the
metal to maintain its bright perfection, and Mercurius is the basic
element that underlies the transformation process.

We may ask: why is it that "the 'thorn in the flesh' is needed" for
further progress in individuation? A simple answer may be that failure
brings you to your knees, and when you are on your knees you may
pray. The greater the failure, the deeper the prayer. But of course failure
does not necessarily lead to prayer and to transformation. Therapists
know all too well that failure often leads to chronic depression, to
continual self-blame and self-judgment, or to endless recrimination
and complaints against others who are taken to be responsible for one's
failure. Many people sink into a bottomless spiral of blame and
accusation, and this Inferno does not lead to an entry into Purgatorio
and upwards to Paradiso. Dante found the way, thanks to the help of
Virgil and Beatrice, the poetic genius and the spiritual anima. In other
words, a crucible is needed in order for failure to lead not only
downwards but also to "progress" and "ascent," as Jung observes.

The crucible is the key to transformation. As Maria Prophetissa
said, "*Unum est vas*" (the vessel is one), on which Jung comments: "It
is a kind of matrix or uterus from which the *filius philosophorum*, the
miraculous stone, is to be born."[8] This "miraculous stone" is the self,
and what the crucible does is to bring about a reversal of perspective
so that the ego is seen from the viewpoint of the self, not the self from
the viewpoint of the ego.

To see failure from the viewpoint of the self instead of from the
viewpoint of the ego constitutes the essential transformation of
failure into an individuation event. In our time—that is in the post-

religious era and its secular cultural expression—depth psychotherapy is one of the few places that offers a temenos for bringing about this transformation.

Let's say: the crucible offered by depth psychotherapy is the complex inter-subjective relationship, which serves as the context for bringing about a reversal of perspective and a transformation from a "failure narrative" to an "individuation narrative." *Azoth*, aka *Mercurius*, as the spirit of the unconscious and agent of the self, leads the way in recasting the failure story into an individuation story by activating the "field" and producing *symbols* in dreams and active imagination, while the hermeneutical art of the therapist will assist in weaving these symbolic elements into a grounded and meaningful life narrative. Hermes enters in three aspects: as activating agent in the inter-subjective field, bringing it life as a dynamic process; as messenger, leading symbols out of the unconscious; and as Hermeneut, inspiring both therapist and patient in the skillful art of translation of symbols into meaning. The therapist and the patient become co-authors of the new narrative.

The question is: Can we arrive at a reversal of perspective where we see the ego from the point of view of the self? The Dalai Lama offers a pithy message of what this might look like: "When you think everything is someone else's fault, you will suffer a lot. When you realize that everything springs only from yourself, you will learn both joy and peace."[9]

Such a reversal comes about through realization that our ego-consciousness lives within a constructed world, made up of interpretations that are mostly based on projection, desire, and expectation, and complex-controlled narratives. The reversal of perspective comes about through the psychological insight into this constructed world and seeing through its illusions. This is the beginning of the reversal.

Jung says something very similar in his comments on the Chinese Rainmaker story, told him by Richard Wilhelm:

> … if one thinks psychologically, one is absolutely convinced that things quite naturally take this way [speaking of the rainmaker's ability to create rain]. If one has the right attitude then the right things happen. One doesn't make it right, it is just right, and one feels it has to happen in this way. It is just as if one were

inside of things. If one feels right, that thing must turn up, it fits in. It is only when one has a wrong attitude that one feels that things do not fit in, that they are queer. When someone tells me that in his surroundings the wrong things always happen, I say: It is you who are wrong, you are not in Tao; if you were in Tao, you would feel that things are as they have to be. Sure enough, sometimes one is in a valley of darkness, dark things happen, and then dark things belong there, they are what must happen then; they are nonetheless in Tao.[10]

A brief clinical vignette: A man in his mid-sixties had suffered a string of significant "failures" over the course of the previous ten years: failures in profession (loss of jobs), failures in relationship, to which were added the deaths of significant others about which he felt some guilt. After many sessions and much reflection on these failures, plus a host of dreams and active imaginations, he one day said, out of the blue, "You know what, through these failures I have been released!" This was an epiphany. By this he meant that he was released from his one-sided and neurotic absorption in his own "failure narrative" and the blaming of self and others that immediately entailed, and he could now begin to construct a very different narrative of his life as he was facing into his final years of life. He had suddenly found the Tao, and this shift in consciousness makes all the difference.

If the individuation process has "laws," then we could almost say that the recognition of defeat or failure of the ego's will to power is the beginning of individuation. This brings you to your knees, and now you can pray. A reversal of perspective becomes possible: "not my will but thy will be done." The narrative is changed from the ego's success/failure cycles and judgments to an individuation story made of light and dark features, and the emergence of the self becomes seen as the main theme of life's development. This does not mean that there is no more ever a sense of failure in life but that each failure becomes taken into the individuation narrative as a further manifestation of the self. The experience of the self is a defeat for the ego, as Jung says, and the defeat of the ego is an experience of the self.

THE COLLECTIVE

We have seen why failure is necessary for individuation on a personal level—it may lead to a reversal of perspective and let us see our lives from the heights of the self. But what about the collective, about nations and cultures, and the world as a whole?

What are the failures to be considered? On a global scale: The success of technology in the modern world threatens to create a catastrophic failure for humanity; the success of colonialism in earlier centuries has ended in failed states around the world; the success of the human species spells failure for the planet and all the other species. These are huge failures and lead us to wonder if we can be saved from ourselves. Will the unconscious save us? Can the self spontaneously defeat us in our determined march toward global failure as a species? Will the self produce compensations that prevent humanity's spiral into fatal and permanent failure? Can humanity individuate?

The beginning would be to see our success as a species on the small planet earth, a tiny speck of dust in the universe, which may itself be a tiny bit of a multiverse, as failure. Once failure is recognized, it can be placed into the crucible and transformed into a new perspective. Can the failure of our species become the entry point into a new sense of meaning within the perspective of a cosmic narrative? Humanity needs a reversed perspective—from blind ego-driven ideas for growth and expansion and technological control over nature to a vision of our place and role among transcendent powers beyond our control. For this reversal we need a crucible, that is, a symbol that reverses the rust of failure into the gold of wisdom. How can we change perspective from collective ego to collective self on a global scale?

Marie-Louise von Franz in her last public lecture, entitled "C.G. Jung's Rehabilitation of the Feeling Function in our Civilization," puts forward her idea of the adequate crucible for reversing our fundamental perspective on a global scale:

> But what are we to do then? Change the policies and, on a deeper level, change our code of laws?—for the latter obviously deals with these questions… Probably it is not the right way to deal with the problem. I think that … we must first really acknowledge the reality of the unconscious (of God, i.e., the Self and of another spirit-world) before we can do anything else.[11]

Awareness of the unconscious and the reality of the psyche would be the crucible of failure on a global scale.

Almost certainly we will fail in bringing about this change in perspective among peoples and cultures that are dedicated to modern and post-modern consciousness. We will fail also with people who have already made up their minds that they know for certain who or what God is and wants, in other words the religiously orthodox. These two groups make up the vast majority of human beings alive on our planet today. Yet maybe we have a chance if we keep at it, in depth psychotherapy on an individual level and with publications and in conferences and media on a collective level. Maybe the insight will grow that we are failing as a species; maybe we will fall collectively to our knees and begin to pray; maybe we will find in the rust the gold of a transformed perspective on the world and ourselves. Anyway, we must try.

NOTES

[1] C.G. Jung, "Religious Ideas in Alchemy," *Psychology and Alchemy*, in *The Collected Works of C.G. Jung*, eds. Herbert Read, Michael Fordham and Gerhard Adler, trans. R.F.C. Hull (Princeton: Princeton University Press, 1968), Vol. 12, § 338. Further references to the *Collected Works*, abbreviated to CW, will be by chapter title followed by volume and paragraph numbers.

[2] *The Holy Bible*, Mark 15: 33-4, New Revised Standard Version, Oxford University Press, 1989.

[3] Harry Eyers, "Triumph of the Spiritual," in *Financial Times*, May 6, 2014.

[4] Author and primary source unknown, "Claudio Arrau, Biography," at http://www.princeton.edu/~gpmenos/biography.html (accessed August 14, 2014).

[5] Jung, "The Conjunction," CW 14, § 778, original italics.

[6] *Ibid.*, "Individual Dream Symbolism in Relation to Alchemy," CW 12, §§ 206-208.

[7] "Azoth," in *Wikipedia, The Free Encyclopedia*, at http://en.wikipedia.org/wiki/Azoth (accessed August 14, 2014).

[8] Jung, CW 12, § 338.

[9] The Fourteenth Dalai Lama, Saying posted January 27, 2014, at *His Holiness the Dalai Lama, Public Figure*, Facebook, https://www.facebook.com/pages/His-Holiness-the-Dalai-Lama/335605676576312 (accessed August 15, 2014).

[10] C.G. Jung, *Visions: Notes of the Seminar Given in 1930-1934*, Vol. 1, ed. Claire Douglas (Princeton: Princeton University Press, 1997), p. 335.

[11] Marie-Louise von Franz, "C.G. Jung's Rehabilitation of the Feeling Function in Our Civilization," in *Jung Journal: Culture & Psyche* 2:2, 2008, p. 15.

7

Even Fairy Godmothers Can Fail

Diane Cousineau Brutsche

No one is shielded from failure. Indeed, even fairy godmothers can fail. Fairy tales abound with stories of failure, and this is the case for the French fairy tale by Charles Perrault, "Donkey Skin" ("Peau d'Âne"), which is the basis of my reflections for this paper. In contrast to most other tales, failure here does not result from the initiatives of an aspiring hero or heroine (who may be said to personify the ego). Rather, failures arise from the advice of a fairy godmother, who symbolizes a spiritual entity, in principle a helpful, benevolent one. So what is the meaning of such advice, which in reality may appear at first to be unconscious blunders or even betrayals? Like the Grimm's "Allerleirauh," Perrault's "Donkey Skin" is about a princess (symbolically, a feminine ego) who is prisoner of her father's incestuous desire. The tale goes on to tell of the princess's successful emancipation after repeated failures. Fairy tales are, of course, archetypal stories, and therefore timeless at any rate. But this tale becomes very contemporary when one approaches it from the point of view of the collective psyche, especially as a representation of the feminine psyche living under the influence of today's patriarchal values and culture.

The Tale

There was a king, the tale begins, who had a faithful and very beautiful wife, and from their union was born a daughter. The king and queen were so happy together that they had no regret having "only a daughter" as heiress to the kingdom. The story continues,

> The palace was magnificent and the stables sheltered a large number of horses. Surprisingly, among these beautiful horses a donkey occupied the place of honor. The fact is that every morning instead of dung, this donkey dropped great quantities of gold coins upon the litter.
>
> One day the queen became very ill and no physician could find the necessary remedy. As she felt her death approaching she made her husband promise that after she died he would remarry only when he found a woman who matched her beauty.
>
> When the queen died the king was inconsolable and his grieving lasted for a long time. One day however his counselors came to him, as they were worrying about the future of a kingdom without a male heir. They urged him to remarry and to try to beget princes as soon as possible, and he finally agreed. As he wanted to keep his earlier promise, he started looking for a princess whose beauty would equal that of his deceased wife. He could find none, until one day he beheld his daughter, who in the meantime had grown up, and he found that she not only equaled his wife's beauty but even surpassed it. So he fell desperately in love and decided to marry her.
>
> When he proposed marriage, the princess got terribly frightened and deeply confused, since a daughter has to obey her father! Not knowing how to solve the problem, she sought the advice of her godmother who was a fairy. The godmother reassured the princess and promised that no harm would come to her if she followed some special advice: The princess was to ask her father, as a condition of marriage, to give her a dress the color of the sky, a request that seemed impossible to fulfill. But the following day a magnificent dress with all the shimmering colors of the sky was delivered to the princess. The godmother's advice

had failed to rescue her. In despair the princess went back to her godmother, who now told the princess to ask her father for a dress the color of the moon. A few days later she received a dress all embroidered with silver and pearls. She got of course even more alarmed. Undeterred by this second failure, the godmother advised her to ask her father for a dress as bright and shining as the sun. Not a week had passed when the princess received a dress woven completely of gold and diamonds. Escape from her father's unnatural desire seemed increasingly hopeless.

But the fairy came again and told the princess to ask her father for something he certainly would not provide: the skin of the magical donkey, the very source of the kingdom's richness. Hardly had the princess asked for it, did the donkey skin land on her bed, and the princess seemed doomed to marry her father. One more failure! And this time certainly, it was the princess's very last chance to avoid a tragic destiny. "Not at all," answered the fairy godmother. "Wait until the night, then wrap yourself in the donkey skin, leave the palace and go to a far away country. Under such a disguise no one will recognize you and they will let you pass." Before the princess left, her godmother gave her a chest containing the three dresses, her jewels, a mirror, and all that is needed for a princess. The godmother assured her that, wherever she would go, from beneath the ground the chest would follow her. Finally she said, "Take this magic wand; tap the ground with it when you need your chest and the chest will appear." The princess obeyed, ran away from the palace during the night, and found refuge in a far distant farm where she was hired to clean out the pigsty.

Every Sunday, when she had time to rest, she locked the door of her little room, washed herself, tapped the ground with the magic wand, put on one of her wonderful dresses, and rejoiced at looking at herself in the mirror.

One day a prince stopped at the farm on his return from hunting. Passing in front of the little room he heard a bit of noise coming from inside. Curious to see who or what was in there, he looked through the keyhole and saw the most beautiful princess, with whom he immediately fell in love. And of course, as it should be, after a series of events he ended up marrying her. The kings from all the neighboring kingdoms were invited to the wedding, and among them was the princess' father, who in the meantime had remarried. He recognized his daughter and asked for her forgiveness.[1]

A happy ending therefore, but only after a succession of failures. From a Jungian standpoint, the tale can be said to symbolize the development of an individual feminine psyche. Moreover it describes a challenge that concerns not only women, but nowadays men as well, quite dramatically. It reveals obstacles we are bound to encounter and potential traps we may fall into. But it also provides us with precious hints for taking up the challenge creatively. I therefore propose to highlight the essential symbolic elements and to follow the development of the tale both on the individual and collective levels, by observing the two in parallel.

Images of Loss, Regression, Incest

The whole drama begins with the Queen's death. In a fairy tale a character's death can symbolize an element of the psyche that has sunken into the unconscious. Seen from the perspective of an individual psyche, this "element" could represent an absent mother, or a mother who shies away from her role, leaving the whole scene to the father, with all the consequences entailed for the child's development. In this tale it is the Queen who dies, therefore symbolizing the loss of a very central feminine archetype. From the standpoint of the collective psyche this disappearance perfectly corresponds with the elimination of the archetypal divine feminine from religious mythologies. It is particularly true of all western monotheistic traditions in which, over the millennia, the god image has come to be an exclusively masculine one. This phenomenon coincides with the development of the patriarchal system that still predominates in every contemporary so-called developed society.

The consequence of a masculine dominance is well described in the tale: The king may personify a powerful masculine entity, or a father, who, for lack of a wife or lack of an anima or inner feminine partner, falls into a deep regression—so much so that his libido turns towards his daughter. He has lost his genuine power and functionally he is neither a husband nor a father any more. The princess herself, motherless and prisoner of her father's desire, typifies the case of father-daughter incest in which the father, while pursuing his aim with abusive paternal authority, proves to be a psychologically infantile man. No psychologically mature man can become an incestuous father.

In the same way, one can postulate that a society in which women are reduced to an inferior status is a society in which men tend to be infantile. Irrespective of the culture of origin, men who feel the need to subordinate women are neither mature nor powerful. To the contrary they are so insecure, so frightened by women, that they cannot relate to them as equals. Therefore to secure their own fragile supremacy they subdue women, often with brute force.

What is also revealing is that as long as the king and the queen were still together they did not regret having "only" a daughter as heiress to the kingdom. Not until the queen's death does the concern with a male heir arise—and when it does, it is under the pressure of the king's councilors. We can understand the situation as such to represent a one-sidedly masculine collective, which uproots the feminine principle from its archetypal fundament, devalues it, and considers it unfit to lead. The tale expresses here very clearly the extent to which the fate of women in society is linked with the loss of the archetypal feminine image.

Now, where a mother is really present and psychologically mature, the stage cannot be easily set for father-daughter incest. This tale, however, reveals a mother's huge culpability, namely in the promise that the queen extracts before her death. In other words, a mother can unconsciously deliver her daughter into the hands of the patriarchy. And one can wonder if discriminatory patriarchal societies could endure without the consent of women, of mothers who raise their daughters to obey the patriarchal rules.

On first sight, the fairy tale might seem to portray a very pathological development, at least until the positive ending. Fairy tales however are, like dreams, symbolic expressions of a psychic reality. So they hold, just as dreams do, paradoxical messages, messages that contain seemingly contradictory, incompatible ideas. They point towards a reality that remains paradoxical and foreign to the rational perspective and the perspective of the conscious ego.

PARADOX AND CREATIVE FAILURES

In order to discover the paradoxical messages of this particular tale, one has to go beyond the potentially tragic situation. So for now, we shall leave aside the concrete, destructive dimension of real life incest, to enter the symbolic dimension and look at what could be happening to a daughter while she remains locked in her father's sphere.

The fairy tale princess acquires three beautiful dresses—gifts from her father that amount symbolically to wonderful qualities corresponding with a daughter's essential psychic needs. Presently we shall turn to the meaning of these dresses. Of course the king's generosity is motivated by his possessiveness, his fatherly will to keep his daughter for himself. But not only does he want to keep her, he even wants to marry her, which sounds very problematic. On the other hand his desire to marry means that he perceives her not only as a daughter but also as a potential queen, a potential woman, a potential equal. Which may explain his readiness to respond to some of her deep inner needs.

Each of the precious dresses given by the king to his daughter could be the matter of many meanings. I will give here only a few possible hints. In fairy tale books, the first dress, described to be the color of the sky, is most often illustrated in blue, a color associated with spirituality, immateriality, the realm of imagination. Here this dress is also said to have a shimmering, therefore changing gleam. One could think for instance of the realm of primary imagination and emotions, a realm of changing moods, but which contains the seeds of creativity. The second dress, the moon dress embroidered with silver and pearls, clearly refers to the feminine as such. So we could say that, thanks to the conflict with her father, this princess perceives herself in her difference, in her feminine identity. In such a gift, a daughter discovers perhaps her inner relationship with Aphrodite, the goddess of love and beauty. Finally the sun dress points to an apollonian mode—the realm of rational thinking, discipline, discrimination—i.e., qualities related to the animus. This dress is the most archetypally masculine gift that the princess receives from her father. Evocative of Athena, born out of Zeus's head, the "sun dress" suggests a powerful feminine logos.

So if the fairy godmother's advice seems to fail from time to time, there may a hidden *telos* or purpose in her methods. For just as garments are symbolically related to initiation rituals, so the princess's acquisition of the three meaningful dresses suggests phases in an overall process that belongs to a girl's coming-to-being as a young adult, well equipped to face further life challenges. But the princess is not set free by her father's gifting of the dresses. As she thus far remains captive in the royal palace, seemingly stuck in hopelessness, we can imagine her as a daughter whose arduously repeated efforts and successes and defeats are all needed for her gaining of the essential psychic qualities.

THE PATERNAL UROBOROS

The late Jungian analyst Erich Neumann helps us to shed light on the psychological meaning of such a situation. Talking about the father's role in the development of the psyche, he stated the absolute necessity for the child to break the early pact with his or her mother and enter the realm of the father. He named this crucial transition the "patriarchal phase."[2] In other words, symbolically speaking, the queen or mother must die to allow the child to become absorbed in what Neumann called the "paternal uroboros."[3] The symbol of the Uroboros, a serpent biting its own tail, can accurately describe a daughter who is "absorbed," as if walled up in her father's "palace." Such absorption is however, according to Neumann, crucial for the psychological development of both male and female individuals. The emerging values in this stage are ego consciousness, individual responsibility, and rationality. Without such qualities, one would remain bound to the archetypal mother and subjugated to the unconscious, lingering indefinitely in a sort of inner still-stand.

Transposing Neumann's statements on this "patriarchal phase" to the collective level, we might well conclude that today's much criticized patriarchy cannot be reduced to an evil reality. We can postulate that it is, on the contrary, a collective manifestation of the father archetype, an essential phase in our collective psychic development. However, by now, most of us are aware that, collectively, we have reached a dramatic dead-end. We find ourselves humanly, economically, and environmentally locked in an impasse as a consequence of a long-lasting, one-sidedly masculine set of values, which practically rule our planet. The creative potential of the patriarchy threatens to become utterly destructive.

The fairy tale provides us with very precious hints about what has led us to such a distressing dead-end, and what could still determine a positive or negative outcome of the disquieting situation in which we find ourselves. The first hint is given in the active presence of a fairy godmother. Symbolically this would mean that the mother image has been positively integrated, a psychological reality that would allow each of us to claim from our fathers and other patriarchal entities all that they can provide for our individual and collective feminine development. Yet among contemporary women there is a wide spread rejection of the traditional mother role, a phenomenon that can be understood as a legitimate refusal to be confined exclusively to a single, imposed role. The consequence however is that this legitimate refusal is often coupled with a rejection of feminine identity as such. In other words, the psyches of such women seem to no longer involve the activity of a "fairy godmother;" no inner voice defies the patriarchal authority or claims recognition of the essential "otherness" and legitimate needs of the feminine.

A GOLDEN CAGE

As precious as they can be, however, none of the three dresses can free the princess from her father's domination. Symbolically speaking, none of the qualities they represent suffice to redeem the feminine psyche, nor are they adequate to take us out of the collective dead end. Indeed each dress entails a potential trap.

For instance, should a girl be content with nothing but the spirituality and imagination associated with the sky-colored dress, she would remain a *puella*, daddy's little girl with an immature ego, lost in a world much too big and threatening for her. She would probably need to find rescue in a husband as soon as possible, and preferably one in the image of her father, a patriarchal husband. In other words she would end up marrying her father, psychologically speaking. Should she get stuck in her fascination for the feminine as such, symbolized in the moon-colored dress, she would reduce herself to the role of an anima figure. Identifying with the anima, her sense of self would be dependent on the mirroring gaze of men.[4]

The third and seemingly most precious dress, all in gold and diamonds, symbolizes the solar, apollonian qualities that enable a young woman to find her way into the larger world, to be professionally successful, to climb ladders just like her male colleagues do. But this "sun dress," probably the most fascinating and seductive of all, can amount to a golden cage. For it contains the allure of the success that is most likely to make us forget about the higher goal of escape, imparted to us as the fairy godmother's ultimate way to heal profound wounds such as those that now afflict much of humanity and nature. This kind of success is a royal trap that often remains ignored by certain trends of contemporary feminism.

A clear distinction has to be made between the needs that pertain to women as a gender group and those needs that concern humanity and nature at this point in our collective history. In other words we should distinguish between women's needs and the feminine values that can be held by males as well as females. As a gender group, women are still heavily suffering from gross discrimination in every contemporary society. Despite many improvements that can be observed over the last few decades, especially in developed societies, it remains an aberrant but persisting phenomenon that women receive inferior wages for equal jobs as compared with their male colleagues; and physical and sexual violence against women still prevails all around the planet, while in many contemporary cultures women are purely and simply stripped of most basic human rights. The battle for women's rights still needs to be carried on, and perhaps for many more generations.

For all those who engage in this fight, the apollonian "sun dress" is an essential asset. However, because the qualities it represents are those needed for social success, it is likely to exert a dangerous fascination. It can indeed lead to an identification with social success, which itself becomes perceived as an ultimate goal instead of a means to other ends. One who lands in this place goes on perpetuating patriarchal values, many examples of which can be found among people holding leadership positions. Be it as the head of a company or a country, patriarchal men and women can remain "locked up in the palace," i.e., conceiving their own value only with reference to masculine standards. As long as one still acts within the walls of the palace, the gifts bestowed by the king remain his own property. Neither can the fullness of one's individual personality be actualized, nor can any of these gifts help to bring us out of the collective dead-end.

This is actually a trap into which both men and women are likely to fall. Sons, just as well as daughters, can be caught in the incest bond. A conversation I had once with a male friend of mine who was at the time in his late forties provides a dramatic example. He had spent his whole life desperately trying to faithfully imitate his very successful father—going so far as to have chosen his father's profession in spite of being typologically very different and miserably unfit for it. I allowed myself one day to ask this friend why he continued to emulate his father instead of searching for his own life. The answer he gave me was flabbergasting. He said, "I prefer being a good photocopy to being a bad original." Hardly believing my ears, I remained dumbstruck. Such possession by the father complex is seldom expressed so painfully. But the complex remains nonetheless very active in the psyches of many individual women and men, and the archetypal father goes on imposing its one-sided rules on the collective psyche, leading us always deeper into the impasse.

In the one-sided patriarchal system the feminine has been "repressed, depreciated or subordinated to masculine ends," says Edward F. Edinger.[5] And so have the qualities associated with it. Edinger continues, "Another change or transition is thus needed to redeem [the] neglected psychic elements."[6] This new phase is what Neumann calls the "integrative phase," an essential phase for both the individual and the contemporary collective.

In his book *The Tao of Physics,* the physicist Fritjof Capra describes the cultural imbalance in contemporary western societies, using the Chinese concepts of *ying* and *yang*. The imbalance, he writes, is characterized by,

> an over-emphasis of all the yang—or male—aspects of human nature, [while] the *ying*—or female—modes of consciousness … have constantly been suppressed in our male-oriented society.[7]

Thus we have emphasized rationality over instinct, power over caring, greed over sharing, profit over human well-being, immediate results over lasting endeavors, science over religion, spirit over nature and matter, ego over soul, and so forth and so on. The challenge consists in finding a dynamic balance between the polarities. But, to again cite Capra:

> To achieve such a dynamic balance a radically different social and economic structure will be needed: a cultural revolution in the true sense of the word. The survival of our whole civilization may depend on whether we can bring about such a change.[8]

Capra wrote *Tao of Physics* in 1975 and yet the same malaise still persists, in spite of innumerable warnings and creative endeavors initiated by men and women who have dared to … wear the donkey's skin.

Conclusion: The Donkey Skin

So here we are, finally back to the title of our tale. The princess finally gains her freedom thanks to the fairy godmother's fourth and last suggestion, which was to flee, hidden in the donkey skin. From the perspective of a patriarchal mind this kind of subversive escape may be easily felt as a failure and very likely to provoke reluctance. The symbol of the donkey is indeed a humble one: it evokes the sense of heaviness, slowness, and even very often stupidity. Having enjoyed the magnificent garbs of power and recognition provided in the "sun dress," more than one woman or man may well shrink from the prospect of such dull fur and unattractive guise—but then, they might fail ... to fail.

However the donkey represents inestimable qualities as well. It is a hard working animal, capable of and willing to carry heavy burdens in the service of human beings. With its "big, funnel like ears that can pick up sound a long way off,"[9] the donkey suggests the capacity for intuition. Renowned for sexual potency, it symbolizes also the psyche's instinctual, sensuous elements.[10] Thus it is not surprising that this animal was sacred to the god Dionysius, the perfect counterpart of Apollo.

Furthermore, the donkey of our tale is said to have defecated gold each morning. This symbolic detail immediately conjures up the goal of the alchemical process: transforming base matter into gold. Thus when the princess agrees to wear the donkey skin—at the fairy godmother's urging—she can be said to submit herself to the alchemical process. Or to put it slightly differently, to wear a donkey skin would be to accept the embodiment of values that are devalued by the collective. Hidden within the donkey skin, the princess is moreover reduced to cleaning pigsties. In alchemical terms such a task evokes the *nigredo*, a painful period in the individuation process, necessary especially for individuals who are too conscious, and who are thus "unconscious of [their] unconscious."[11] This particular condition of (un-)consciousness describes accurately the psychological state of an individual who lives in a "patriarchal palace," while repressing or confining to the "stable" the creative energies of the shadow, the instincts, and precious aspects of the psyche associated with the feminine. Our integration of such energies necessitates a phase of withdrawal. We find ourselves in a liminal space, a space of transition in which we are no longer what we were and not yet what we are called to become. Genuine integration requires a painful letting go of previous values, certitudes, possibly even our authentic creative energies. It can and usually does trigger a distressing experience of decline. Any individual who has gone through a deep reassessment of his or her familiar values, ambitions, and convictions knows very well how this feels. And to endure such a trial without shunning away from it, we need both the defiant voice of a fairy godmother—and also the sturdiness and stubbornness of the donkey.

The path however does not end here. Having renounced her high position in the palace and relinquished the associated qualities and values, the princess undergoes a period of restoration, which takes the form of her Sunday rituals. As she washes herself, dons her precious dresses, and gazes at her reflection in the mirror, she progressively discovers her full royal identity. With such insight one can begin to genuinely own the qualities received from the patriarchy and bring them all to the next phase of life.

Likewise a multitude of men and women have abandoned the patriarchal main-stream and applied their acquired masculine know-how in service to a healthier future that points to improvement in the realms of human being, ecology, economy, and soul. Leaving the patriarchal palace as such always entails acceptance of the donkey skin, i.e., a willingness to enter into the *nigredo*, a phase inevitably associated with any deep reassessment of the values still held by collective patriarchal consciousness.

The aim of the *nigredo* or liminal phase is to prepare the psyche for the next phase, represented in the tale by the marriage of the princess and prince. Without this marriage the tale would be meaningless. It can of course symbolize the union of the masculine and feminine polarities in the individual psyche—but it also suggests the triggering of transformations on a wider scale. For the princess's father, who attends the wedding along with the kings of the neighboring kingdoms, has in the meantime remarried. So we can say that after a period of paternal, incestuous regression the masculine and feminine can re-unite and regain their healthy, adult relationship and mutual status within the community as a whole. A new era can begin, as we see thanks to the image of a princess who has freed herself from imprisonment in the patriarchal palace, found her rightful place, and impacted the very world that she had chosen to leave.

This detail has a meaning also for each one of us. Indeed, a world view shaped by contemporary quantum physics coincides more and more with the teachings of mystical traditions. It acknowledges the fact that we are all embedded in a cosmic web and that the whole is influenced by any transformation, even if it be the most modest one taking place in any one part of the cosmos. In other words, we are not powerless: each of our tiniest integrative steps has a global impact. Such a perspective allows optimism, even in the face of the most disquieting prognoses concerning the future of our planet.

"Donkey Skin" is a very rich fairy tale, which most of the time, if not always, is interpreted from the point of view of a girl's or woman's psyche. Even if this approach is understandable it nevertheless eradicates the tale's universal scope. The tale presents us indeed with archetypal processes that concern every human psyche, both women's and men's. We are all children of the patriarchy and like the princess of the tale, each one of us is invited to follow a transformative process and contribute to the creation of an urgently needed new paradigm.

NOTES

[1] My summary and paraphrase, drawing primarily on Charles Perrault, "Donkeyskin," *The Complete Fairy Tales of Charles Perrault* (New York: Clarion Books, 1993), pp. 108-116.

[2] Erich Neumann, *The Child: Structure and Dynamics of the Nascent Personality*, Karnac Classics, trans. C.G. Jung Foundation for Analytical Psychology Inc., reprinted (London: H. Karnac Books, Ltd., 2002), p. 89.

[3] Erich Neumann, *The Origins and History of Consciousness*, trans. R.F.C. Hull, Bollingen Series XLII (Princeton: Princeton University Press, 1973), p. 18. This is one of many books and chapters in which Neumann uses the expression, "patriarchal uroboros."

[4] Marie-Louise von Franz, *The Feminine in Fairytales* (Dallas: Spring Publications, 1972), p. 2.

[5] Edward F. Edinger, "An Outline of Analytical Psychology," originally published in *Quadrant*, a Publication of the Jung Foundation

for Analytical Psychology Inc., Number 1: Spring 1968, reproduced in, *CAPT Center for the Application of Psychological Type*, at http://www.capt.org/using-type/c-g-jung.htm (accessed January 27, 2014).

[6] *Ibid.*

[7] Fritjof Capra, *The Tao of Physics* (Berkeley, CA: Shambala Publications, 1975), p. 160.

[8] *Ibid.*, p. 340.

[9] Ina Woolcott, "Coyote, Power Animal, Symbol of Wisdom, Family Orientation, Illumination," in *Shamanism*, at http://www.shamanicjourney.com/article/6146/coyote-power-animal-symbol-of-wisdom-family-orientation-illumination (accessed January 27, 2014).

[10] Jean Chevalier and Alain Geehrbrant, *The Penguin Dictionary of Symbols*, trans. John Buchanan-Brown (Penguin Books, 1996).

[11] Gerhard Adler, *Studies in Analytical Psychology* (London: Routledge, 1999), p. 19.

About AGAP, ISAPZURICH, and the Jungian Odyssey

AGAP, the Association of Graduate Analytical Psychologists, was founded as a Swiss-domiciled professional association in 1954 by the American, Mary Briner, and several other international graduates of the C.G. Jung Institute Zürich. AGAP is a charter member of the International Association for Analytical Psychology (IAAP). In 2004, AGAP delegated its IAAP training right to a sub-group of some ninety members who in turn founded the International School of Analytical Psychology Zürich (ISAPZURICH). Thus, since 2004, ISAPZURICH has been AGAP's postgraduate training program in Analytical Psychology.

Since 2006 the Jungian Odyssey has taken place each semester as an off-campus week-long retreat, open not only to the students of ISAPZURICH, but also to all with interest in C.G. Jung. In keeping with the Homeric journey, the Odyssey travels from year to year, finding "harbor" in different Swiss "ports." A hallmark of the Jungian Odyssey is its thematic inspiration from the *genius loci*, the spirit of each place we choose.

ISAPZURICH was honored to begin collaborating with Spring Journal Books in 2008, when Nancy Cater proposed the publication of an annual series based upon each year's Odyssey lectures. The inaugural volume, *Intimacy: Venturing the Ambiguities of the Heart*, was published in 2009, ensuing from the Jungian Odyssey 2008. Now with the seventh and final volume in the series, *The Crucible of Failure*, a fruitful collaboration comes to an end. And as we reflected in that last Odyssey, endings, like failures, in their very disruption often hold the promise of even more fruit-bearing than we might ever imagine.

The Jungian Odyssey Annual Conference and Retreat	Venue	JO Series
2006 Jungian Psychology Today: Traditions and Innovations & The Quest for Vision in a Troubled World: Exploring the Healing Dimensions of Religious Experience	Flüeli-Ranft	
2007 Exploring the Other Side: The Reality of Soul in a World of Prescribed Meanings	Gersau	
2008 Intimacy: Venturing the Uncertainties of the Heart	Beatenberg	Vol. I, 2009
2009 Destruction and Creation: Facing the Ambiguities of Power	Sils Maria	Vol. II, 2010
2010 Trust and Betrayal: Dawnings of Consciousness	Gersau	Vol. III, 2011
2011 The Playful Psyche: Entering Chaos, Coincidence, Creation	Monte Verità	Vol. IV, 2012
2012 Love: Traversing Its Peaks and Valleys	Flüeli-Ranft	Vol. V, 2013
2013 Echoes of Silence: Listening to Soul, Self, Other	Kartause Ittingen	Vol. VI, 2014
2014 The Crucible of Failure	Grindelwald	Vol. VII, 2015

All published volumes of the Jungian Odyssey Series can be ordered online at www.springjournalandbooks.com.

Editors

Series Editors

Ursula Wirtz, PhD, Academic Chair of the Jungian Odyssey, is a training analyst and graduate of the C.G. Jung Institute Zürich (1982), maintaining her private analytical practice in Zürich. She received her doctorate in philosophy from the University of Munich and her degree in clinical and anthropological psychology from the University of Zürich. She has taught at a number of European universities, and authored numerous publications on trauma, ethics, and spirituality, which have been translated into Russian and Czech. She has lectured worldwide and taught at various European universities. Her book, *Trauma and Beyond: The Mystery of Transformation,* was published in the Zürich Lecture Series for Analytical Psychology by Spring Journal Books, 2014. She is a faculty member of ISAPZURICH, and a trainer with developing Jungian groups in Eastern Europe.

Deborah Egger, MSW, is a training, supervising, and founding analyst of ISAPZURICH with a private practice in Stäfa. Born in Little Rock, Arkansas, she moved to Zürich in 1986 to train at the C.G. Jung Institute in Küsnacht, and remained in Switzerland having met her husband here. They raised two children and various animals (cats, turtles, rabbits, guinea pigs, and a dog named Twinkle!). She was President of the Association of Graduate Analytical Psychologists (AGAP) for nine years, in this role serving also for six years as a member of the Executive Committee of the International Association for Analytical Psychology (IAAP). Her BA degree is in Religion and Psychology and she holds an MSW in clinical social work. Her analytic areas of focus are in adult development and relationships and transference.

Katy Remark, PhD, received her diploma from the C.G. Jung Institute in 2003 and is now a member of ISAPZURICH. Besides working as an analyst, she is also a Certified EMDR Therapist, a Certified Imago Relationship

Therapist, and has studied and trained in body-centered psychotherapy. Her professional interests include the use of visualization and the somatic pathway in working with assertiveness, anger, aggression, and panic. She maintains a private practice in Zürich.

Stacy Wirth, MA, born in North Carolina (1954), has lived in Switzerland since 1979, when she joined the man who would become her Swiss husband. At the time she carried on her previous work as a dancer and choreographer, and went on to raise two daughters. In the interim she received her MA in the psychology of art from Antioch University (1997), and completed her training at the C.G. Jung Institute Zürich (2003). From 2004-2013 she served on the AGAP Executive Committee. She is a co-founder and training analyst of ISAPZURICH, a member of the Advisory Board of *Spring Journal*, and a Jungian analyst with a private practice in Zürich.

Consulting Editor

Nancy Cater, JD, PhD, is the editor (since 2003) of *Spring: A Journal of Archetype and Culture*, the oldest Jungian psychology journal in the world, and the author of the book *Electra: Tracing a Feminine Myth through the Western Imagination*. She is the publisher of Spring Journal Books, which specializes in books by leading scholars in depth psychology, the humanities, and cultural studies. She is an Affiliate Member of the Inter-Regional Society of Jungian Analysts, a former appellate court attorney, and lives in New Orleans, Louisiana.

Contributors

Diane Cousineau Brutsche, PhD, was born in Montreal, Canada and earned a doctorate in French literature from the University of Paris. She is a graduate of the C.G. Jung Institute Zürich and has been in private practice in Zürich since 1992. She is a training analyst and supervisor at ISAPZURICH. Among her publications in English are "Betrayal of the Self, Self-Betrayal, and the Leap of Trust: The Book of Job, a Tale of Individuation," in *Trust and Betrayal: Dawnings of Consciousness, Jungian Odyssey Series*, Vol. III (Spring Journal Books, 2011); "Instigating Transformation," in *Jungian Psychoanalysis: Working in The Spirit of C.G. Jung* (Chicago: Open Court, 2010); "Lady Soul," in *Spring: A Journal of Archetype and Culture, Symbolic Life*, Vol. 82, 2009; and *Le paradoxe de l'âme: exil et retour d'un archetype* (Geneva: Georg éditeur 1993).

Andrew Fellows, PhD, is a Jungian analyst with private practices in Bern and Zürich, a deep ecologist and writer, and has served on the Program Committee of ISAPZURICH. He holds a doctorate in applied physics, and has two decades of international professional engagement with renewable energy, sustainable development, and environmental policy. His special interests include the *anima mundi*, the mid-life transition, the new sciences, the I Ching, and the use of depth psychology to understand and address global collective problems, especially climate change. His lifelong passions include mountaineering, taijiquan, and music.

Ursula Lenz Bücker, Dr. med., studied psychiatry, trained as a psychotherapist, and for nearly twenty years has been in private practice as a specialist in psychosomatic medicine, homeopathy, and palliative care. In 2003 she received her diploma from the C.G. Jung Institute Zürich, and went on to become a training and supervising analyst at ISAPZURICH. She has lectured on shame and trauma, and held seminars on active imagination and the expression of inner processes by using creative arts.

Renos K. Papadopoulos, PhD, is Professor of Analytical Psychology at the University of Essex, where he is also the Director of the Centre for Trauma, Asylum and Refugees, and a member of the Human Rights Centre. He is as well Honorary Clinical Psychologist and Systemic Family Psychotherapist at the Tavistock Clinic. In addition, he is a training and supervising Jungian psychoanalyst and systemic family psychotherapist in private practice. As consultant to the United Nations and other organizations, he has been working with refugees, tortured persons, and other survivors of political violence and disasters in many countries. He lectures and offers specialist training internationally, and his writings have been published in twelve languages. Forthcoming: *Involuntary Dislocation: Home, Trauma, Resilience and Adversity-Activated Development* (Routledge). See also, for example: "Ethnopsychologische Annäherungen an Überlebende von Katastrophen. Prolegomena zu einer jungianischen Perspektive," in *Analytische Psychologie. Zeitschrift für Psychotherapie und Psychanalyse*. Heft 172, 44. Jg., 2/2013; and "The *Umwelt* and Networks of Archetypal Images: a Jungian Approach to Therapeutic Encounters in Humanitarian Contexts," in *Psychotherapy and Politics International*, 2011, Vol. 9, Number 3.

Bernard Sartorius, lic. theol., received his degree in theology from Geneva University in 1965 and worked for several years as a protestant minister, first in a parish and then in youth work. He graduated from the C.G. Jung Institute Zürich in 1974, maintaining his private analytical practice first in Geneva, and since 1997 in Lucerne and Zürich. He is a training analyst and supervisor at ISAPZURICH. Among his publications on symbolical subjects are the essays, "The Silence of 'God,'" in *Echoes of Silence: Listening to Soul, Self, Other*, JOS Vol. VI (Spring Journal Books, 2014); "Eros and Psyche Revisited," in *Love: Traversing Its Peaks and Valleys*, JOS Vol. V (Spring Journal Books, 2013); "La Mecque où/ou on meurt," in *Vouivre, Cahiers de* *psychologie analytique, Pèlerinages,* Numéro 11, 2011; and his book on the orthodox church, *L'Eglise orthodoxe, Grandes religions du monde,* Vol. 10 (Edito-Service, 1982).

Murray Stein, PhD, Canadian born, completed his university education in religion and psychology in the USA, and trained at CGJI-ZH. Today he is a training analyst and supervisor at ISAPZURICH, where he previously served as president. He is a former president of the International Association for Analytical Psychology (IAAP) and a founding member of two IAAP societies: the Inter-Regional Society for Jungian Analysts (USA) and the Chicago Society of Jungian Analysts. He has authored many books, including *Jung's Treatment of Christianity* (Chiron, 1985), and the forthcoming *Minding the Self: Jungian Meditations on Contemporary Spirituality* (Routledge, 2014). He is the editor with Jean Kirsch of *How and Why We Still Read Jung: Personal and Professional Reflections* (Routledge, 2013). With Nancy Cater he is co-editor of the *Zurich Lecture Series in Analytical Psychology* (Spring Journal Books), which follows the weekend of lectures co-hosted every autumn by Spring Journal Books and ISAPZURICH.

Polly Young-Eisendrath, PhD, is a psychologist, mindfulness teacher, writer, and Jungian analyst who maintains a clinical and consulting practice in central Vermont. She came to psychology and Jungian training through the doorway of Buddhist practice, taking formal Zen vows in 1971. Polly has published on couple relationships, women's development, parenting, and psychotherapy practice— aiming at practical applications of the insight and wisdom gained from psychology, psychoanalysis, meditation, and self-awareness. Polly is Guest Editor of *Spring: A Journal of Archetype and Culture, Buddhism and Depth Psychology: Refining the Encounter,* Vol. 89, 2013. Her essay, "Jung and Buddhism: Refining the Dialogue" appears in *The Cambridge Companion to Jung,* 2nd Ed, edited by Polly and Terence Dawson (London: Cambridge University Press, 2008). Among her many other publications are: *The Self-*

Esteem Trap: Raising Confident and Compassionate Kids in an Age of Self-Importance (Little, Brown & Co., 2009); *Women and Desire: Beyond Wanting to Be Wanted* (Three Rivers, 2000); *The Resilient Spirit: Transforming Suffering into Insight and Renewal* (Da Capo, 1997). Her most recent book is a memoir: *The Present Heart: A Memoir of Love, Loss and Discovery* (Rodale, 2014). It details her discoveries about love in losing her beloved husband, Ed Epstein, to early onset Alzheimer's Disease.

Lightning Source UK Ltd.
Milton Keynes UK
UKOW06f1953270515

252413UK00001B/5/P